Critical Guides to French Texts

58 Constant: Adolphe

Critical Guides to French Texts

EDITED BY ROGER LITTLE, WOLFGANG VAN EMDEN, DAVID WILLIAMS

CONSTANT

Adolphe

Second edition

Timothy Unwin

James Barrow Professor of French
The University of Liverpool

Grant & Cutler Ltd
1996

© Grant & Cutler Ltd
1996
ISBN 0 7293 0388 8

First edition 1986
Second edition 1996

DEPÓSITO LEGAL: V. 4.287 - 1995

Printed in Spain by
Artes Gráficas Soler, S. A. - La Olivereta, 28 - 46018 Valencia
for
GRANT & CUTLER LTD
55-57 GREAT MARLBOROUGH STREET, LONDON W1V 2AY

Contents

Preface

ITALICIZED numbers in parentheses refer to items in the Select Bibliography at the end of this volume. References to the text of *Adolphe* are to the Folio edition *(7)*. Quotations from other works by Constant are taken from the Pléiade selection *(1)* ; however, the *Journal* entries are, for convenience, identified by their date alone.

This study draws upon many ideas and insights from other works, and it is not possible to detail its sources exhaustively. A small number of recent works on *Adolphe* has been added to the Select Bibliography in this reprint, but the student should be aware that there are many other useful items to be found through the standard bibliographical sources. *Adolphe* continues to attract critical attention, both because of the tragic plight it describes, and because of Constant's exemplary handling of the subtleties of confessional narrative. The studies carried out by the late Alison Fairlie in the 1960s are, however, still the most penetrating and lucid material available, and I would urge my own readers to read or to re-read her central trio of articles (listed in the Select Bibliography). My own debt to them is no doubt obvious.

I wish to record here my thanks to all those who helped in the preparation of this volume, and to those who made suggestions on the first printed version of it. For this reprint, a number of small changes have been made, but the text remains substantially the same as the earlier one. My special thanks go to the generations of students who, year after year, have given me proof of the continuing relevance and challenge of Constant's text. I dedicate this volume to one student who was so confronted by *Adolphe* that she gave up her studies and set about changing her life. May her story have had a happy ending.

July 1995

Introduction

Few novels can be more elusive than Constant's *Adolphe*. Encouraged by the very tone of the work to enter into the process of moral judgement, the reader is thwarted in all attempts to arrive at unambiguous conclusions. The conflicting assessments of the character of Adolphe which come at the end of the novel are an obvious reminder of its ambivalence: whilst an indulgent view will tend to minimize the harm inflicted by the hero, a harsh view will underestimate his qualities of compassion and lucidity. Nor does there seem to be any manner of reconciling these judgements, since there is a point at which Adolphe's strengths and weakness can be seen to coincide, compassion becoming synonymous with capitulation, lucidity with indecision. If we feel tempted to condemn him, we must not forget that it is he who has provided us with the wherewithal to accuse; and if we wish to condone, we must remember that the very act of confession invites complicity. The tension between precise psychological and moral insights, and the open-ended values implicit throughout the work, is central to the experience of reading *Adolphe*. It accounts in part for those reactions of anger and frustration which are common among students and professional critics alike.

To defend a work of art which causes anger and frustration might be less of a paradox than first it appears. There are many examples of artists who set out to provoke precisely those negative feelings which are essential to the expression of their message. Who has not at some time bristled with righteous indignation on reading La Rochefoucauld, and thus been faced with first-hand evidence of the working of 'amour-propre'? If we experience frustration on reading *Adolphe,* it is easy to see why this is necessary to the

world-view offered within the work: for frustration is born
of the clash between the desire for moral clarity and the
sense of the unending complexity of the issues. In a work
which suggests the existence of absolute moral laws, we find
ourselves obliged to accept an uncomfortable sense of freedom. *Adolphe*, perhaps more than any other work of the
Romantic period, sounds the note of existential anguish
familiar to the reader of Sartre or Camus. The hero of
Camus's *La Chute* might be seen as a literary descendant of
Adolphe. He too will have the sense that there is no longer a
ready-made set of values to cling to, and he will hasten his
own spiritual fall by his desire to understand and analyse. In
a discarded fragment for prefaces to the second and third
editions of *Adolphe* (1816 and 1824), Constant describes this
destructive form of self-consciousness and suggests that it is
central to his subject when he writes:

> J'ai voulu peindre dans Adolphe une des principales
> maladies morales de notre siècle: cette fatigue, cette
> incertitude, cette absence de force, cette analyse
> perpétuelle, qui place une arrière-pensée à côté de
> tous les sentiments, et qui par là les corrompt dès leur
> naissance. (*4*, p. 304)

Frustration may, then, be considered a legitimate and
desirable reaction (initially at least) in the reader of
Adolphe: it should not be considered a proof of the work's
moral futility. It is only when we begin to accept the
possibility of successive reinterpretations of the text (thus
becoming more self-conscious ourselves as readers) that its
message begins to operate. The great variety of themes
suggested within it – love, sincerity, self-analysis, language,
society, death and religion (to name but the most prominent) – should not deceive us into thinking that Constant is
simply having his say on a series of separate issues. Rather,
these are interdependent facets of a world-view which
stresses complexity above all and which incorporates within
itself a variety of different standards of judgement. The
novel does not fail to provide insights: but it implies that

any conclusions which may be drawn are a function of
context (textual, social, historical) and must therefore by
their very nature be provisional. As Flaubert was later to
write: 'La bêtise consiste à vouloir conclure'.[1] The statement might have met with some sympathy from Constant,
insistent as he was on the multiplicity of truth and on the
relevance of the apparently secondary theme or detail. As
he wrote in his *Journal* on 10 December 1804:

> Tout ce qui exerce l'esprit est bon, et il est même
> dangereux à quelques égards de trop rechercher si le
> but est utile. A force de ne vouloir que l'utilité, on
> élague mille choses dont on méconnaît l'utilité indi-
> recte. Tout se tient. Aucune vérité, aucun fait, aucune
> face nouvelle d'une idée n'est absolument isolée. (*I*, p.
> 390)

To study *Adolphe* is to discover how the text operates as
an organic entity, full of echoes, reversals, structural sym-
metries and counterpoints, the richness of which gives the lie
to the apparent bareness of much of the language used. To
look at the work initially in terms of its construction and its
technical qualities is thus the most appropriate way into its
message. And as recent criticism has increasingly stressed,
once it is accepted aesthetically then the moral and philosophical problems begin to resolve themselves: for that is
the level at which Constant's shifting, open-ended vision of
the world best operates.

---

[1] Letter to Louis Bouilhet, 4 September 1850, *Correspondance*, Paris,
Gallimard, vol. I, 1973, p. 680.

Part One

Organization of the Text

1. GENESIS

WHEN Constant writes in the preface to the second edition of his novel that 'aucun des caractères tracés dans *Adolphe* n'a de rapport avec aucun des individus que je connais' (p. 25), he is perhaps taking a deliberately simplistic stance on the question of lived experience and its fictional reworking. That there were biographical origins to the novel is beyond doubt, but that the basic data underwent a considerable transmutation in the process of writing is something which a wary author might have considered his critics incapable of understanding.

The immense distance between lived experience and literary form was confirmed by the publication in the 1950s of formerly undisclosed material: the text of Constant's unfinished novel *Cécile,* and the full text of the *Journaux intimes.* Far from enabling scholars to find direct correlations between the novel and the author's own life, these texts (taken in conjunction with *Adolphe*) show the progressive reworking of biographical data. While the *Journaux intimes* reveal the details of Constant's emotional vacillations, together with a first, provisional attempt to transcend these through the written word, *Cécile* is clearly at a further remove from real life. Based on the biographical data of Constant's liaison and eventual marriage with Charlotte de Hardenberg and his inability to break with Madame de Staël, it is more noticeably fictional in its approach. The use of a retrospective first-person narrator, the paring down of detail, the alterations to real characters and the changing of names, together with the emphasis on chronological progression towards a foreseen result – this all suggests that

Constant is working towards a more artistic and less biographical goal, however thinly the biography may as yet be disguised. But it is in *Adolphe* that the biographical particulars are finally and fully subjected to the logic of aesthetic creation, and where the generalized philosophical framework goes beyond the details of lived experience. We are confronted by an exemplary tale, of relevance to all.

This does not mean that biographical fact is excluded from *Adolphe*. It is quite in order that there should be an overlap between artistic creation and lived experience, provided that the latter is integrated into the conception of the work. If we accept that Constant comes anywhere near to this, then to read the novel as an exercise in self-revelation becomes an almost entirely irrelevant approach, since it speculates at several removes on the raw material. There are, of course, obvious attractions: a biographical approach might, if it were to add some psychocritical weaponry to its arsenal, speculate that the death of Ellénore is an instance of wish-fulfilment on the part of Constant himself, as he engages in the imaginary destruction of Madame de Staël; it might reinforce its argument by saying that this 'death by a broken heart' would otherwise appear to be a cliché. But looked at in purely aesthetic terms, Ellénore's death has an obvious and necessary place in the text: from the outset death is one of the major concerns of the novel, and Ellénore's physical death is the correlative of Adolphe's spiritual death. A strictly textual approach to such matters will give a more truthful picture of the way in which the author has organized and developed his theme.

The fact that some of Constant's material is biographical in nature meant that criticism of the novel was dominated for almost a century and a half after its first publication in 1816 by speculation on what lay outside the text. Great was the lure to see in the character of Adolphe a portrait of the author himself; greater still that to find the source of Ellénore, held by some to be based on Madame de Staël and by others to be based on Anna Lindsay. [2] The material of

---

[2] See Delbouille (*14,* pp. 114-20) for a detailed account of this debate.

the *Journaux intimes* now makes it abundantly clear that no single woman can be seen as the key to the character of Ellénore. The same themes return in many of Constant's relationships: the sense of intense arousal when faced with sexual refusal, the *but-lien* theme, and the complex interdependence of submissiveness and revolt. If, in the present state of criticism of *Adolphe*, there is still room for an analysis of the link between biographical fact and completed text, it must be along the lines of demonstrating how Constant uses art as a form of therapy or transcendence of self: an approach which has been adopted in two notable studies of recent years *(24, 33)*. But if writing does perform this function for Constant, then the implication is that the link with his own life is severed and that the work must stand or fall on its intrinsic merits.

Yet the problem of the relation of *Adolphe* to biographical fact cannot be laid to rest until we have looked at the circumstances of its composition. The first reference in the *Journal* comes on 30 October 1806 (a full ten years before the novel's eventual publication). In one of those episodes of his life which seem to prefigure Proust's 'intermittences du cœur', Constant has fallen anew for his old flame Charlotte de Hardenberg. He writes: 'Ecrit à Charlotte. Commencé un roman qui sera notre histoire. Tout autre travail me serait impossible'. Initially, the novel in question appears to be an enthusiastic treatment of this renewed love – something very different, it would seem, from the eventual subject of *Adolphe,* and rather closer to that of *Cécile.* But ten days later comes the first reference to an episode containing a character called Ellénore: 'Avancé mon épisode d'Ellénore. Je doute que j'aie assez de persistance pour finir le roman' (10 November 1806). Thereafter, Constant refers both to an 'episode' and to a 'roman'. At first they appear to be quite separate but subsequently the 'épisode' seems, in its turn, to become the 'roman'.

Now this raises some difficult questions. First and most obviously, what is the relation between episode and novel, and why the initial distinction? Second, is there a link

between the novel as conceived at the outset and the story of
Cécile as we now know it? If so, how did Constant imagine
bringing together the two stories, and at what point – and
why – did he decide on their separation? Without becoming
over-involved here in that favourite scholars' topic, the
genesis of *Adolphe* and *Cécile*, there are two points I would
like to make by way of clearing the ground in order to look
at *Adolphe* as it stands in its definitive form. [3]

The first is this. Despite the attractiveness of the hypothesis that the 'roman' referred to in Constant's journal is in
fact *Cécile*, we cannot assume this to be the case. The
reason is simple: the internal chronology of *Cécile* leads up
to 2 February 1808, a period well after the one we are
talking about. We might wish to argue as some critics have
done (see especially *4,* pp. lxvii-lxviii) that *Cécile* was begun
concurrently with *Adolphe* but continued much later. This
would certainly satisfy the natural wish to see a progression
in Constant's technique, as he breaks from the biographical
constraints of *Cécile* and turns to a more truly artistic
approach in *Adolphe*. But the hypothesis might prove too
tenuous for some.

This leads to the second point. Whether we believe
Adolphe to have been written prior to *Cécile*, concurrently
with it or subsequently to it is only of secondary importance. The overriding fact is that it is clearly at a further
remove from the reality of Constant's life, and represents a
greater degree of stylization. Ellénore contains qualities of
tenderness and submissiveness which in *Cécile* are the attri-
butes of two different women: apart from making her a
more convincing character, this lends dramatic concentration to the novel. What is noticeable, even at an early stage
in the composition of *Adolphe*, is that Constant shows signs
of being concerned with aesthetic questions. After the initial, uncritical enthusiasm as he writes about Charlotte, he
takes cognizance of the artistic shortcomings of his first few
days' work: 'Lu mon roman le soir. Il y a de la monotonie.

---

[3] On the genesis of *Adolphe* and its relation with *Cécile* see Delbouille
(*14,* pp. 34-60).

Il faut en changer la forme' (4 November 1806). Could it be that the breakaway episode which becomes the story of Ellénore is conceived as a means of adding variety and interest to the story? Certainly, it is apparent that Constant soon finds qualities in this episode which were not present in what he called the novel. He writes on 12 November: 'Lu le soir mon épisode. Je la crois très touchante,[4] mais j'aurais de la peine à continuer le roman'. Some time later, when he reads his story to M. de Boufflers, Constant's remarks in his journal suggest first that the resemblance to real life is still too great, and second that it would be advisable to leave Ellénore as the only female character. The aesthetic considerations now appear to be gaining force:

> Lu mon roman à M. de Boufflers. On a très bien saisi le sens du roman. Il est vrai que ce n'est pas d'imagination que j'ai écrit. *Non ignara mali.* Cette lecture m'a prouvé que je ne pouvais rien faire de cet ouvrage en y mêlant une autre épisode de femme. (Le héros serait odieux.) Ellénore cesserait d'intéresser, et si le héros contractait des devoirs envers une autre et ne les remplissait pas, sa faiblesse deviendrait odieuse. (28 December 1806)

Two remarks ought to be added. First, the author's own suggestion that his story has its basis in reality should not be taken as an invitation to see nothing else in it. The worry that it is lacking in imagined content is a natural and salutary concern on the part of the novelist, who after all seems to have altered his material after this reading of it. Second, it is obvious that even at this stage of the composition of *Adolphe* the author wishes the motivation of the story to be credible in its own terms, hence the decision to leave out the other 'épisode de femme'. Clearly, questions of structure, proportion and internal coherence are beginning to dictate the orientation of the work.

---

[4] Constant systematically puts the word 'épisode' in the feminine. This is contrary to normal usage.

2. ACTION AND REFLECTION

Where a novel with biographical origins aspires to the
expression of a universal message, we should expect to find
in it (as we do in *Adolphe*) a consistent process of distilla-
tion and concentration. The reality of its starting-point is
transcended not only by the alteration or exclusion of naked
fact, but also by the imposition of an overall artistic and
philosophical pattern (the latter is apparent even if one has
no knowledge of the biographical starting point). There are
two areas of truth here – that of art, and that of life – and
whereas they may merge together, they will ultimately
remain separate. In a passage of Gide's *Les Faux-Monnayeurs,* the distinction between the two, and the area
of common ground, are defined with striking clarity when
Edouard, an aspiring novelist and in a number of respects
the author's own mouthpiece, describes his admiration of a
scene in Racine's *Mithridate:*

> Parfois il me paraît que je n'admire en littérature rien
> tant que, par exemple, dans Racine, la discussion
> entre Mithridate et ses fils; où l'on sait parfaitement
> bien que jamais un père et des fils n'ont pu parler de
> la sorte, et où néanmoins (et je devrais dire: d'autant
> plus) tous les pères et tous les fils peuvent se recon-
> naître. [5]

To put it another way, Edouard is saying that the truth of
life is that of personal experience; the truth of art, on the
other hand, lies in that generalizing power which is able to
find the common strand in separate manifestations of similar themes, whilst at the same time giving immediacy and
relevance to its portrayal.

Applied to *Adolphe*, this idea gives an insight into the
type of 'truth' we might be looking for. Whereas in Constant's diaries the tergiversations and traumas of daily existence are noted with all the spontaneity of immediate

---

[5] André Gide, *Les Faux-Monnayeurs,* Paris, Folio, 1977, p. 184.

suffering, the gradual progression of *Adolphe*, based on pivotal moments which both epitomize what has preceded and prefigure what is to follow, has that exemplary quality of all great art. But there is in addition a paring down of detail, an alertness of language and a careful selection of what is most expressive in the context. Developments in the action take second place to the overall effect which the author is seeking to create.

Let us look at one small instance of this process which is at the very heart of Constant's achievement. When Ellénore, having regained her father's property in Poland, tries to provoke her lover's jealousy by encouraging the advances of other men, Adolphe's outrage at her manœuvres is suggested with the deftest of touches. 'Je m'expliquai vivement avec Ellénore: un mot fit disparaître cette tourbe d'adorateurs', writes the narrator (p. 102). In a short, bare paragraph everything is angled towards the result of this event: nothing need be given of the content of the dispute between the lovers, the point of overriding importance being that its apparent resolution leads only into a further impasse. When Ellénore has acted to disperse this group of gallants, the sickening consequence is suggested through the blunt symmetry of the two final phrases of the paragraph: 'Ellénore se croyait de nouveaux droits; je me sentais chargé de nouvelles chaînes' (p. 102). Action has been reduced to a minimum and is reported with the utmost simplicity. We are confronted not by the reality of 'life' but by the artifices of a text. The careful structuring which is in evidence beneath the surface of the action tends to give to each episode of *Adolphe* that paradigmatic quality which Gide's would-be novelist will so admire in *Mithridate.*

The subjugation of detail to a role of secondary importance; the superimposing of reflection and generalization upon the particulars of the action: we might at first be tempted to see this as the standard procedure of any narrative where he who tells the tale is also he who lived through it. The decision to narrate presupposes an intelligence of past events. What is different about *Adolphe* is that the process is taken much further than is usual. To the Aristote-

lian notion of the 'imitation of an action' is added reflection
upon that action and interpretation of it within the 'drama'
itself. Crucial, in this respect, is the presence of maxims
throughout the text evoking the complexity of human behaviour, for they remind us constantly of the narrator's wish to
see events from a higher perspective. In a sense, we have the
simultaneous presence of two things, described by Edouard
in *Les Faux-Monnayeurs* as: 'd'une part la réalité, [...]
d'autre part cet effort pour la styliser'.[6] Now I do not wish
to pretend that *Adolphe* is some kind of new novel 'avant la
lettre', for the maxim, with all its connotations of worldly
wisdom, had also been a significant feature of the eighteenth-century novel. Yet Constant's own use of the maxim
also anticipates that blending of action and reflection which
we see in later novelists such as Flaubert and Proust. His
narrator, who seems at once to remain aloof from his
past experience (which he judges and analyses) and to
re-enter his earlier perception of things, points the way
forward to the ambiguous narrator of Flaubert's novels,
infiltrating the subjective world of the characters and discreetly articulating their dreams, then standing back and
offering a rational (often cruel) assessment. As with Flaubert, the line of demarcation between the character's
thoughts and the narrator's comments seems almost impossible to draw: both as the hero of the story and as its
narrator, Adolphe possesses cerebral and analytical qualities
which push him towards generalizations about his own
experience. The maxims which occur throughout *Adolphe*
thus become a focal point in the tone of the work, towards
which all reflection is directed. They are the final fruition
of Adolphe's attempts to understand his own behaviour. As
such they give, on the philosophical level, that quality of
universality to the work; and on the stylistic level, they lend
tautness to the narrative through the manifold recurrence of
similar formulae.

It would be quite possible to remove some of Constant's
maxims from the text and to allow them to stand alone. So

---

6 *Les Faux-Monnayeurs,* p. 185.

detached is their tone that, like the maxims of La Rochefoucauld, they can be seen to offer a self-contained and coherent statement: 'Les sentiments de l'homme sont confus et
mélangés...' (p. 42); 'Il n'y a point d'unité complète dans
l'homme...' (p. 47); 'L'amour n'est qu'un point lumineux...'
(p. 56); 'La dissimulation jette dans l'amour un élément
étranger...' (pp. 70-71); and many others. Here we find a
parallel with Proust, whose own use of the maxim is well
known.[7] As is the case with Proust, however, the fact that
these maxims can readily be isolated from their context
should not deceive us into thinking that they are artificially
inserted. Although Constant's maxims may often be without
syntactic moorings, they are always introduced with great
care through successive degrees of generalization (for a
detailed analysis of this process see *17*, pp. 230-32).

It is not only such series of graded generalizations which
give the maxim its privileged status in *Adolphe*. Alongside
it, and throwing it into relief, are many half-formulated
attempts at detached insight. These instances of what is only
a partial achievement of wisdom reveal that the narrator is
locked in a continuous and not always successful struggle to
stand back from the particular events of his past and
establish what is universal within them. An illustration of
this might be found in the episode where Adolphe, speaking
of his separation from Ellénore when he leaves the town of
D*** to return to his father, reflects on the pain of departure: 'Il y a dans les liaisons qui se prolongent quelque chose
de si profond!' (pp. 72-73) The exclamation mark here
denotes that his insight is still enslaved (linguistically, emo-
tionally and philosophically) to a particular series of events
and feelings, and that the positive lesson of mutual understanding based on full acquaintance is not yet fully appreciated. This adds an irony to his narration, for the lesson is
clearly there.

Then there is a process of a similar kind to this partial
detachment, but which operates at a further remove: it is the

[7] On Proust's maxims see Justin O'Brien, 'Marcel Proust as a moralist',
Romanic Review, 39 (1948), 50-69.

presence of a certain reflective trait within the hero at the base-level of his story, that is to say in the samples of direct speech which we are given and through which the narrator is by-passed. When Adolphe, in an episode in chapter six, attempts to tell Ellénore that he no longer loves her, he first offers a definition of love which is perhaps the clearest example in the story of his tendency to analyse and to generalize even before he becomes the narrator. As he says: 'L'amour, ce transport des sens, cette ivresse involontaire, cet oubli de tous les intérêts, de tous les devoirs, Ellénore, je ne l'ai plus' (p. 81). The unusual rhythm of this sentence, where the emphasis is all the more violently thrown on those last words for their having been inordinately delayed, is reminiscent of the technique of 'enjambement' in poetry, where the 'rejet' often concentrates stress at the beginning of a new line. The irony here is that Adolphe, attempting delay in circumlocution before that unintentionally emphatic denial of love, finds that a precise definition of what love should be has fallen from his lips. The remark, though tied to a specific context, is a sign pointing in the direction of reflection and interpretation, and it too reinforces the dominant role of the maxim.

The broadening of perspective allowed by the presence of maxims is not, then, an artificial element welded on to Adolphe's account of his liaison with Ellénore. It has its roots within the very nature of the relationship, and yet we see it returning at almost every level of discourse (even in the letters which conclude the novel). The maxim pinpoints phases of transition or periodic returns of similar dilemmas, and thus provides that blend of differentiation and similarity which is a major part of aesthetic enjoyment. It provides also the sense of inexorability which gives the text its tragic dimension. We have the feeling through the inclusion of the maxims that, when all else fails, there does at least remain the dignity of lucidity. This proud view of human intelligence situates Constant in a tradition which includes such writers as Pascal and Malraux.

The tendency towards philosophical abstraction, constantly in conflict with the data which it attempts to synthesize, thus forms a part both of the aesthetic and the moral purpose of *Adolphe*. Just how pervasive a technique this is is confirmed when we see that it is used not only by the narrator and his earlier self, but also by a number of other characters. At certain points through the novel, trenchant and alarming insights by others offer a counterpoint to the hero's own abstractions. I am thinking, for example, of Ellénore's 'Vous n'avez que de la pitié' (p. 78); or of Adolphe's father's 'Ce n'est plus vous qui la protégez, c'est elle qui vous protège' (p. 86), a remark which ironically makes use of the antithetical structure favoured by Adolphe himself; or of the baron de T***'s reminder to the hero that there is 'entre vous et tous les genres de succès, un obstacle insurmontable, et que cet obstacle est Ellénore' (p. 88). Whilst such utterances are far from having the universality of the maxim, their status as detached observations puts them in a germane category.

This neat process of counterpoint raises the whole question of language and discourse in Constant's novel. We are aware of a fundamental irony which was surely intentional. Whereas the narrator should, by definition, retain the initiative in his own story, Adolphe increasingly becomes the passive object of others' interpretations. It is as though they are telling him his story, rather than he recounting theirs. The irony is doubled when we reflect that these incursions into the narrative usually herald a crisis or a turning-point, whereas Adolphe's own generalizations rarely have such a motivating function (the latter are frequently followed by a switch from present to past historic, and a return to the details of the account). The process reaches its climax in the closing stages of the novel, where the interpreting initiative is posthumously passed to Ellénore. Her letter has been described by one critic as 'la clef de voûte du livre' (*13*, p. 220) in that it represents the point of transition between 'récit' and 'commentaire' (a tension which is at the heart of Adolphe's own narration).

The extent to which the plot of this novel is motivated by the clash between different styles of discourse, and indeed by the problem of language itself, has of course been

stressed by many critics (e.g. *19, 31*). The achievement of
such critical approaches has been to scotch the naïve assumption that, for Constant, writing might involve the
transcription of some fixed and pre-existent reality. If he
depicts his characters as having their view of reality mould-
ed by words, then the implication is that he, the novelist, is
no more able to stand outside language than they are. The
use of the maxim, on the one hand suggesting the existence
of absolute moral laws, on the other hand offers yet another
verbal representation of the world. It epitomizes the conflict
(which we see throughout *Adolphe*) between the urge to find
truth and the awareness that it can never be expressed other
than by a series of approximations and/or linguistic substi-
tutions.

3. PARALLELS AND REVERSALS

If the periodic return of the maxim in Constant's text
provides that satisfying blend of sameness and progression,
there are other levels on which such a pattern operates.
Both at the surface level of tone and at the underlying level
of themes and imagery, the work is organized round a series
of carefully wrought parallels and reversals.

One of the most obvious examples of this attention to
structure is in the successive portraits we receive of Ellénore
in chapters two and eight. The first, when Adolphe has just
met his future mistress, begins: 'Ellénore n'avait qu'un
esprit ordinaire', and ends with the delicate introduction of
the nature theme which is later to assume importance: 'On
l'examinait avec intérêt et curiosité comme un bel orage'
(pp. 44-45). The second portrait is given when Ellénore,
having decided to open up the doors of her late father's
house, fails through over-eagerness to be a social success:
'Elle avait l'esprit juste, mais peu étendu', writes the narrator, who concludes his account with a restatement of that
inner conflict in her character: 'Il y avait dans ses actions et
ses paroles je ne sais quelle fougue destructive de la considération qui ne se compose que du calme' (p. 98). The

placing of the substantival 'calme' at the end of this second portrait provides a link with the word 'orage' of the first, and the transition in Adolphe's attitude is thereby discreetly suggested. The point may be extended to the portraits as a whole. The measured tones of the earlier one, whose factual character is reinforced by the frequency of the straight subject-verb construction ('Elle avait...', 'Elle attachait...', 'Elle était...', 'Elle repoussait...', etc.), are replaced in the second one by more emotive rhetoric. In the middle of the passage we will find a double exclamation: 'Que de dégoûts elle dévora sans me les communiquer! Que de fois je rougis pour elle sans avoir la force de le lui dire!' The fairness of Adolphe's first judgement gives way, in this second portrait, to a more embittered view suggesting signs of continued conflict between the lovers. Whereas earlier he had claimed that despite the average nature of Ellénore's intelligence, 'ses idées étaient justes', now he asserts that 'la justesse de son esprit était dénaturée par l'emportement de son caractère'. In the first case, the narrator halts his account, as he pauses and reflects on the character of his heroine. In the second case, the air of detachment is less genuine, and the portrait is worked into the onward movement of the narrative.

There are many such instances of passages in Constant's novel which, as in a novel by Flaubert or Proust, bear a distinct structural relation to much earlier or much later passages – thus increasing our sense·of the work's close-knit thematic texture. One critic has devoted a brief article to a particularly striking example of two symmetrical yet contrasting moments: these are the crystallization of Adolphe's love for Ellénore at the end of chapter three, and the point of its final loss when the death of Ellénore is imminent.[8] In both cases, the narrator describes his feelings with reference to three things: the presence of other people, the air he breathes and the awareness of nature. In the first case he writes: 'Je marchais avec orgueil au milieu des hommes;

---

[8] See Norman Shapiro, 'The symmetry of Benjamin Constant's *Adolphe*', *The French Review,* 34 (1960-61), 186-88.

[...]. L'air que je respirais était à lui seul une jouissance. Je m'élançais au-devant de la nature' (p. 59). And in the second case we read: 'L'air que je respirais me paraissait plus rude, les visages des hommes que je rencontrais plus indifférents; toute la nature semblait me dire que j'allais à jamais cesser d'être aimé' (p. 114). Sceptics might wish to argue that the recurrences are coincidental, particularly as the three things are not referred to in the same order. But even if this were the case, what is important is that the text none the less remains faithful to its own idiom and operates as a coherent whole. From the reader's point of view, the conscious intentions of the writer himself are all but irrelevant.

In the same category as the above example one might rank two dinner scenes in the novel. The first is when Adolphe is entertained in Ellénore's presence by the comte de P***; the second is when he is entertained in her absence by the baron de T*** (chapters two and nine). The first of these gentlemen presides unwittingly over the beginning of the liaison with Ellénore (as Adolphe writes: 'Quand nous sortîmes de table, nos cœurs étaient d'intelligence'); the second officiates calculatingly over its end (Adolphe tells him: 'Je le prends, l'engagement de rompre avec Ellénore'). In the first scene, painful embarrassment at not knowing how to behave towards Ellénore is followed, on the comte de P***'s intervention, by a sense of relief and social ease (pp. 50-52); in the second scene, the feeling of isolation and the fear of gossip are cast aside when the baron de T*** exercises his social skills and takes the young man under his wing (pp. 103-6). The latter, with 'l'ascendant de sa considération', is to Adolphe what the comte de P*** was in the earlier passage to Ellénore ('Il mettait un grand prix à lui maintenir dans la société la place que son caractère méritait'). Not only does this suggest parity between Adolphe and Ellénore, it also reveals similarities and contrasts between the two noblemen. Both have social assurance and show what they consider to be benevolence towards a person of lower status. But the baron de T*** is clear-sighted and knows where his behaviour is leading, whereas the comte de P*** is heading for a misfortune which he cannot foresee.

Together with the pairing of separate episodes in *Adolphe* there is also the progressive return to the same problems in a fresh context. An example of this might be seen in Ellénore's behaviour towards menfolk in society. Ironically her attitude will turn full circle. First, she encourages the company of men when, after admitting Adolphe into her company, she fears the advancement of his love (chapter three); later, after her separation from the comte de P***, she finds that men seek out her company of their own accord, despite the fact that she now has the opposite wish – to be alone with Adolphe (chapter five); finally, she encourages the company of men once again, this time to try to effect through sexual provocation a new development in her relationship with Adolphe (chapter eight). It is of interest to note that the latter episode, although present in the 1810 manuscript of *Adolphe,* did not figure in the first edition of the novel in 1816; it was, however, reinstated by Constant for the 1824 edition, now considered the standard one in most respects.[9] The decision would seem to be an implicit recognition of the important role fulfilled by this episode. Apart from bringing to life another facet of the character of Ellénore, it offers a fruitful point of comparison with the two earlier passages. If she encourages the company of men once again, it is this time for very different reasons, and there has been an important change in her character from self-protection to recklessness. On each occasion, her behaviour towards men is determined by her attitude towards Adolphe, which represents the common strand in the progression. An ironic counterpoint to this is Adolphe's own refusal to change his behaviour in society. In

---

[9] A case has, however, recently been made for a composite edition of *Adolphe*, based on the original 1816 edition but with the informed inclusion of later variants. See C.P. Courtney's introduction and edition (37).

chapter five, when Ellénore is pestered by male hopefuls, his attitude is ambivalent: 'Tandis que je repoussais avec l'indignation la plus violente la moindre insinuation contre Ellénore, je contribuais moi-même à lui faire tort dans mes conversations générales' (p. 71). The double-talk will persist when, in spite of his wish to speak well of Ellénore in the presence of the baron de T***, Adolphe again attacks her indirectly through generalizations: 'Je parlais en riant des femmes et de la difficulté de rompre avec elles' (p. 104).

The parallels and contrasts which emerge from an attentive reading of Constant's novel are enhanced by the occasional transfer of attitudes, aspirations or modes of behaviour from one character to another. We have already seen how Adolphe's use of the generalized statement is sometimes turned against him, and how the initiative of interpretation is wrested from him by Ellénore in her final letter. But there is also transfer of more strictly psychological dispositions. It is Adolphe, for example, who strives throughout for resignation. Ellénore who rebels against submission; yet in the end it is Ellénore who, against all the odds, comes closest to that attitude of acceptance which has eluded the hero. The momentary peace experienced by Adolphe at the end of chapter seven as he contemplates the nocturnal scene is the nearest he will get to a detached view of his situation; but although at first surprised and relieved to discover that he still possesses 'la faculté de m'oublier moi-même', he begins to succumb again to despair even as he continues his walk ('Ah! renonçons à ces efforts inutiles...', pp. 93-94). Ellénore, however, reopens the question of resignation as she approaches her death: 'Comme la nature se résigne!' she exclaims on beholding the winter landscape. 'Le cœur aussi ne doit-il pas apprendre à se résigner?' (p. 112). From that moment forward she moves closer to an attitude of serenity, and although a note of agitation will persist to the last, she entertains no new hopes of a rebirth of her relationship with Adolphe, and remains firm and dignified in her final hours. It is Adolphe who is left with that sense of remorse and despair which earlier had been hers. It is noticeable too that, whilst it was initially Ellénore who had tried to resist change in her relationship with Adolphe – even before her separation from the comte de P*** she was saying 'Gagnons des jours, gagnons des heures' (p. 63) – by the end of the novel it is Adolphe who is wishing that time would freeze, as with horrified impotence he contemplates Ellénore's deterioration.

4. LANGUAGE AND IDIOM

The impression of economy and tautness which we have on reading Constant's text is increased by the very language he uses. Although we may initially be tempted to see the language of *Adolphe* as abstract,[10] there is on the contrary frequent use of physical vocabulary to convey moral impressions, or alternatively of vocabulary which, whilst abstract in its normal usage, acquires physical connotations by its positioning in the text. It is possible to find on almost any page of *Adolphe* a striking proportion of words in these categories. They may not, on a computer word-count, be the most frequent ones (a list of these will be found in *14*, pp. 272-73), but they are distinguished by their emphatic function. Examples of such words are: *serrer, arracher, blesser, déchirer, lutter, plier; contraction, obstacle, peine, douleur, contrainte, effort, agitation; violent, déchirant, pâle, amer, froissé* (this very incomplete list omits, in particular, many of the more prominent verbs). In the light of this, one begins to see the care which has been taken over what might appear to be throwaway phrases on a first reading: '...faute de s'être *pliée* à des convenances factices, mais nécessaires' (p. 37); 'en *lutte* constante avec sa destinée' (pp. 44-45); 'je n'avais jamais éprouvé de *contraction* si *violente*' (p. 51); 'elle m'*arracha* la vérité' (p. 77); 'elle se *précipitait* de nouveau dans la coquetterie avec une espèce de *fureur*' (p. 101); '...encore *froissé* de la *douleur* que j'avais éprouvée'

---

[10] One particularly harsh contemporary wrote of Constant's novel that it was riddled with 'patois philosophique' and 'jargon sentencieux' (*La Quotidenne,* 31 July 1816, quoted in Delbouille, *14*, p. 396).

(p. 105); and so on (the italics are mine). The more one
looks for such vocabulary, the more one discovers how
central to the text is the idiom of physical constraint and
struggle. It is so insidious, and yet so easily overlooked at
first, that when we discover it our reading of the text might
almost, for a while, be deformed by the awareness of its
continuous presence.

What must be kept in perspective when one looks at the
physical vocabulary of *Adolphe* is the view of human nature
implicit within it: life is a struggle for self-domination, a
struggle which may involve moments of violent embarrassment or pain, and which in the most extreme cases can lead
to the moral or physical destruction of an individual. In
this sense the first chapter of the novel (which some see as
the hardest to justify in terms of the underlying unity of the
work) does much to establish the idiom of struggle with the
self, and in the death of the old lady who had been
Adolphe's first intellectual mentor it offers a prefiguration
of the conclusion. It is worth noting that the narrator
underlines the energy and resistance of this woman, whose
particular response to outside social pressure was to stand
firm in her own convictions ('La vieillesse enfin l'avait
atteinte sans la soumettre'). But finally the effort of resistance was itself too much, and the narrator tells us: 'J'avais
vu la mort la frapper à mes yeux' (p. 38). Ellénore too will
show a proud resistance in her final struggle, and the
narrator emphasizes the vigorous persistence of one facet of
her personality when he writes: 'Un seul sentiment ne varia
jamais dans le cœur d'Ellénore: ce fut sa tendresse pour moi'
(p. 113). The two portrayals of physical death in the text
are, then, linked by the same idea, the second being an
amplification of the first.

But there are responses to the struggle for self-
domination other than defeat or death, and the text offers a
variety of different manners in which the sense of inner
constraint or agitation is expressed. Even before the sketch
of the old lady, the narrator describes an alternative reaction
in the attitude of his father who, on the one hand wanting to
unburden himself, and on the other hand embarrassed by

the thought of self-revelation, finds relief in the outlet of
cynicism or irony. This prefigures Adolphe's own erratic
behaviour in social circles, which varies between patient
compliance and destructive sarcasm. On other occasions,
the impact between complex inner feelings and external
pressures finds no solution at all and stops dead with a
sudden feeling of 'étonnement' (another of those words
which occasionally play a key role in *Adolphe*). When the
narrator talks of his first contact with society, he draws
attention to 'l'étonnement de la première jeunesse, à l'aspect
d'une société si factice et si travaillée' (p. 40). Later, there is
an echo of this reaction in the sketch of Ellénore's children
'portant sur leurs visages cet étonnement de l'enfance lorsqu'elle remarque une agitation dont elle ne soupçonne pas
la cause' (p. 64). The characters for whom such inner
conflict is least marked in the novel are in fact those whose
social identity demands that they bypass the anarchy of
personal feelings. This is most true of the baron de T***,
described as 'un vieux ministre dont l'âme était usée, et qui
se rappelait que, dans sa jeunesse, il avait aussi été tourmenté par des histoires d'amour' (p. 104). It is also true
at first of the comte de P***, whose self-confidence is
however shattered by the departure of Ellénore. Within the
small compass of this novel, the reader is confronted by an
impressive diversity of reactions around the basic idea of the
struggle with self.

Then there is the related theme of military strategy and
encounter: for the struggle for self-mastery is a battle both
with oneself and, if necessary, with others. Nowhere is this
idea more fully integrated into Adolphe's idiom than in the
pages which describe his seduction campaign: 'Ellénore me
parut une conquête digne de moi', he writes (p. 45), and a
little later: 'Je formais mille projets; j'inventais mille
moyens de conquête' (p. 47). But when the campaign is
thwarted by a combination of Adolphe's own timidity and
the inappropriateness of circumstances, it becomes interna-
lized: he talks, for example, of 'les combats que j'avais livrés
longtemps à mon propre caractère' (p. 48). Herein lies the
distinctive nature of Constant's treatment of the theme.

Whereas *Adolphe* appears to be in the libertine tradition
of earlier novels like *Les Liaisons dangereuses,* the idea
of military strategy is much more than an external code of
practice. It is an integral part of Constant's very vision of
man, and the struggle for domination of others exists in
continuum with the struggle for victory over oneself. In the
very chapter where we read of Adolphe's strategy to con-
quer Ellénore, we also discover that she seems locked in
some internal conflict. It is even that conflict which lends
to her some of her charm, for as the narrator tells us: 'Ses
idées semblaient se faire jour à travers les obstacles, et sortir
de cette lutte agréables, plus naïves et plus neuves' (p. 46).
Later, a more conscious side to the struggle will emerge
when Ellénore, 'par un calcul faux et déplorable' as Adolphe puts it, will try to provoke her lover's jealousy; and
believing that her plan has worked, 'elle s'applaudit de son
stratagème' (p. 100). But the battle will be extended to
include both main characters, vying for power over each
other and finding themselves in stormy confrontation. 'Les
scènes recommençaient sur un autre terrain', says the narrator (p. 100). And a little later in this episode of the eighth
chapter, when the original military campaign is degenerat-
ing into wanton destruction: 'Il n'y eut plus même entre
nous ces retours passagers qui semblent guérir pour quelques instants d'incurables blessures' (p. 102). Whether it be
in the internal struggle for self-mastery, or in the outer
strategies developed as a means to dominate others, or even
in the conflicts which such strategies produce when pursued
on two sides, the vocabulary of military confrontation is an
important facet of the language of this novel.

There are, beyond the domain of purely military vocabulary, further extensions of the idiom of conscious man-
œuvre and calculation in the text. Alongside the word
'stratagème', there is a synonym for it which figures with
equal prominence: 'calcul'. It denotes the conscious and
artificial provoking of situations from which a character
hopes to gain some advantage. We see it in the 'calculs et...
systèmes' of Adolphe's seduction campaign (p. 47), or in the
manœuvres by the baron de T*** to separate the lovers ('le

cruel avait trop bien calculé...', p. 110). Opposed to those moments of calculation are other moments where some powerful, elemental feeling seems to take over. After the return of Ellénore and prior to his conquest of her, the young Adolphe once again senses an inner wholeness, undisturbed by conscious psychological artifice: 'Il n'était plus question dans mon âme ni de calculs ni de projets' (p. 52). Ellénore's love for Adolphe is precisely of this wholesome type: 'Elle s'était relevée à ses propres yeux par un amour pur de tout calcul, de tout intérêt' (p. 62), and it is one of the ironies of the novel that this sense of integrality should persist in the heroine but come only in fits and starts to the hero. Adolphe thus finds himself calculating in respect of his own feelings, and his luckless attempts to intensify his sense of attachment to Ellénore underline the falsehood of the position he is in. As he writes of his fading love after Ellénore's separation from the comte de P***: 'Que peut, pour ranimer un sentiment qui s'éteint, une résolution prise par devoir?' (p. 70). The idea of calculation is not confined to the attempts to out-manœuvre others; it is linked with the whole problem of the role played by the conscious mind in the creation or destruction of emotions.

5. IMAGERY

The language of conflict and struggle is reinforced in the text by a number of striking images. These fall broadly into three groups (although, as we shall see, the divisions are not watertight). First there are images of captivity; then images of light and darkness (with the added connotation of life and death); and finally, images of nature.

The image of captivity becomes precise and explicit at the point in the novel where, as Adolphe walks alone through the countryside at night, he reflects on all that he is deprived of through his enslavement to Ellénore. Praise for his abilities, he says, seems a cruel reminder of his subjugation: 'Je croyais entendre admirer les bras vigoureux d'un athlète chargé de fers au fond d'un cachot' (p. 90). (The

suggestion of darkness is important here, as it is throughout
the passage. It will be discussed under the second series of
images listed above.) Later, when Ellénore has given up the
company of would-be suitors in response to Adolphe's
anger, the image again returns in an explicit manner: 'Ellénore se croyait de nouveaux droits; je me sentais chargé de
nouvelles chaînes' (p. 102). But these two clear allusions to
captivity have been prepared long in advance, for Adolphe
has consistently emphasized his own submissiveness and his
mistress's power. At the outset of the liaison, he had written
to her of the sense of oppression and shame from which he
hoped to escape by the symbolic entry into her house:
'Quand je touche au seuil de votre porte, quand je l'en-
tr'ouvre, une nouvelle terreur me saisit: je m'avance comme
un coupable, demandant grâce à tous les objets qui frappent
ma vue' (p. 58). In the event, entry into her house will turn
out to be servitude rather than freedom, a twist which is
ironically foreshadowed when Adolphe, by way of explaining Ellénore's attachment to him, contrasts his own 'soumis-
sion' towards her with the comte de P***'s attitude of
condescension (p. 59). But Adolphe's subsequent dissatis-
faction will be voiced within precisely the same terms of
reference as those in which he expressed his joy at the
beginning. Whereas formerly he had talked of spending
'quelques heures à ses pieds, me proclamant le plus heureux
des hommes' (p. 56), later he will complain: 'Elle me
poursuit partout, comme un esclave qu'on doit ramener à
ses pieds' (p. 106). The image of servitude, followed through
the text, is an effective pointer to this transition in Adolphe's attitude.

The imagery of light and darkness in the novel is
perhaps more thorough and more extensive. The symbolism
of light as knowledge and truth, darkness as ignorance and
falsehood, has of course been in existence for about as long
as writing itself. Constant's own twist to the theme comes
through the ambivalent attitude which emerges towards the
'light' of knowledge, for knowledge can also be destructive.
In one of the most lengthily developed images in the novel,
we are confronted with precisely this connotation:

> C'est un grand pas, c'est un pas irréparable, lorsqu'on
> dévoile tout à coup aux yeux d'un tiers les replis
> cachés d'une relation intime; le jour qui pénètre dans
> ce sanctuaire constate et achève les destructions que la
> nuit enveloppait de ses ombres: ainsi les corps ren-
> fermés dans les tombeaux conservent souvent leur
> première forme, jusqu'à ce que l'air extérieur vienne
> les frapper et les réduire en poudre. (p. 96)

The passage epitomizes the ambiguity of Adolphe's situation. Whereas light represents the truth of external knowledge, it is also the catalyst of destruction; and if darkness is
the domain of ignorance and death, it is also a refuge and a
sanctuary. The image is delicately poised between these
conflicting implications, thereby avoiding the clichés into
which it might so easily have fallen, and contributing to the
sense of inextricable complexity suggested by the text as a
whole.

Elsewhere in the novel the idea of darkness, although
retaining its primary association of unwisdom or blindness,
also has the opposite connotation where it is seen as a
welcome release from self-scrutiny. This is how it is presented in the passage describing Adolphe's night of wandering in
chapter seven. Together with the advent of night comes the
feeling of nature's peace, and Adolphe escapes from that
petty introspection which is the very source of his malaise:

> Les ombres de la nuit qui s'épaississaient à chaque
> instant, le vaste silence qui m'environnait et qui
> n'était interrompu que par des bruits rares et lointains,
> firent succéder à mon agitation un sentiment plus
> calme et plus solennel. (p. 92)

During this scene, awareness of suffering and of self will be
prompted, not by darkness, but by the perception of light,
whether it be a lamp in the window of a house which
produces the reflection that there 'quelque infortuné s'agite
sous la douleur' (p. 93), or whether it be the return of
daylight which focuses Adolphe's thoughts once more on
Ellénore. All this is despite the fact that the night which

envelops Adolphe is explicitly linked for him with thoughts of death. The irony is that this retreat into the darkness is, for a while at least, an escape and a release rather than a confrontation; but the ambiguity is retained by the fact that, even from his precarious serenity, Adolphe relapses into anguish in the latter stages of his meditation.

The ambiguity attaching to the idea of darkness in this single passage of the novel might be traced, in the case of images of light, in separate and contrasting passages. One of these is the celebration of love which opens chapter four, and another is the final walk taken by the dying Ellénore in chapter ten. In the first passage, love and light are equated in a traditional way, as Constant writes of 'ce jour subit répandu sur la vie, et qui semble nous en expliquer le mystère' (p. 60). Taken with the statement a few pages earlier that 'l'amour n'est qu'un point lumineux, et néanmoins il semble s'emparer du temps' (p. 56), it would appear to be the corollary that all that the lovers need fear is the return of darkness. Yet the very opposite is suggested in the scene describing the final walk, as the pale winter sun shines weakly upon the earth: 'C'était une de ces journées d'hiver où le soleil semble éclairer tristement la campagne grisâtre, comme s'il regardait en pitié la terre qu'il a cessé de réchauffer' (p. 112). As Georges Poulet has pointed out (*26*, p. 51), the sun here is like Adolphe's own lucidity; it can illuminate but brings no warmth. Light is no longer seen as the source of joy and life; it is the cold, implacable observer of impending death. The light of Adolphe's love for Ellénore has now become the cold light of truth.

Of the nature-images in the novel, it is perhaps that of the storm which is most central and most apparent. But before discussing it, I should like to mention three other aspects of the natural scene which are repeatedly evoked: the air, the flowing or arid spring, and dead or infertile vegetation.

We have already come across a number of examples, in other contexts, of references to the air. Adolphe breathes it with triumph when he has seduced Ellénore, with a sense of its harshness when her death is imminent; air combines with

light to destroy bodies in their tombs in the image previous-
ly discussed. There are many deliberate and pointed references to the act of breathing throughout the text, emphasiz-
ing the link between a natural element and the intimate
emotions of characters. From Adolphe's 'un air qui pénètre
dans ma poitrine oppressée' (p. 57), through to the descriptions of the dying Ellénore when we are told that 'sa
respiration fut moins oppressée' (p. 111) or that 'sa respiration devint plus lente' (p. 116), we are confronted consistently with the dichotomy of joy and life versus pain and
death. Thus a central theme of the novel is reinforced by a
discreet undercurrent of natural imagery.

The allusion to a flowing or arid spring might be
considered rather predictably symbolic of the success or
failure of self-expression. Constant's use of the image is,
however, deft and delicate and, as is sometimes the case
with other images, only one explicit reference is needed in
order to bring alive a number of phrases used elsewhere in
the text. When we are told of the relationship between the
lovers that 'la source des longs entretiens était tarie' (p. 97),
we may recall a word used much earlier in the novel, when
Adolphe had described his conversations with the old lady
who was his first mentor as 'inépuisables' (p. 38). We may
also recall, in another context, the words uttered by Ellénore when she refuses to travel to Poland without Adolphe:
'Je souffre déjà suffisamment par l'aridité de vos manières et
la sécheresse de nos rapports' (p. 83). Linking with the idea
of the spring, yet also ushering in the storm-image, is that of
the torrent. When Adolphe reminisces on his childhood he
finds that 'mille souvenirs rentraient comme par torrents
dans mon âme' (p. 91); or, when reflecting on the suffering
inflicted by life and on the need for the hope offered by
religion, he asks: 'Au milieu du torrent qui nous entraîne,
est-il une branche à laquelle nous osions refuser de nous
retenir?' (p. 115).

Just as the image of the spring ultimately relates to that
of the storm, so too do images of vegetation. At the end of
chapter six, where Adolphe describes his attempts during
the journey to Poland to recapture the language and the

emotions of love, we read: 'mais ces émotions et ce langage ressemblaient à ces feuilles pâles et décolorées qui, par un reste de végétation funèbre, croissent languissamment sur les branches d'un arbre déraciné' (p. 85). The tree would, one presumes, have been uprooted by natural causes such as lightning or a flood: in other words, by a storm. But the emphasis here is on some empty and prolonged calm after the storm; it is the deathly and funereal hush that descends on Adolphe's love, where only a few languid leaves now testify to earlier strength and vigour.[11] This dramatic image prefigures something of the effect of the final winter scene, where frost has stilled the countryside and no life, apart from the couple themselves, is visible: 'Les arbres étaient sans feuilles; aucun souffle n'agitait l'air, aucun oiseau ne le traversait: tout était immobile, et le seul bruit qui se fît entendre était celui de l'herbe glacée qui se brisait sous nos pas' (p. 112). The connotations of the previous image are here reversed: whereas the primary association is now of lifelessness and emptiness, there is a powerful secondary association – for Ellénore at least – of peace and serenity. The barrenness of nature, symbolic of the undoing of hope and the fading of emotions, finally comes to signify something potentially more positive. Faced by the destruction of her love, Ellénore is able to find a measure of calm and to move in the direction of a solution to her inner conflict.

But it is in the image of the storm – to which the other nature-images are secondary – that the most extensive effects are obtained by the author. The ravages and destructions wrought by storms are traditionally symbolic of lovers' quarrels, but two things distinguish Constant's approach: first, the fact that the storm is already suggested by association in other aspects of the natural scene described in the novel; second, the fact that the very character of its heroine is presented in terms of the storm-image ('On l'examinait

---

[11] Another interpretation of this passage is offered by Martha N. Evans in *'Adolphe's* appeal to the reader', *Romanic Review,* 73 (1982), 303-13. Following the Freudian tradition, she sees the uprooted tree as a symbol of castration epitomizing Adolphe's inability to use language productively.

avec intérêt et curiosité comme un bel orage', p. 45). As the fitful and explosive temperament of Ellénore emerges more powerfully under the stress of her relationship with Adolphe, only a few delicate touches are needed by the author to suggest the effect of a storm brewing. 'La conversation avait pris une direction orageuse', he writes of the scene where Adolphe announces to Ellénore that he is staying in D*** for a further six months. The momentum of the image is maintained with an even subtler touch a few lines on: 'La scène devint violente. Nous éclatâmes en reproches mutuels' (p. 65). At the half-way point in the novel, we read of the heroine as she sees through her lover's blandishments: 'Sa figure se couvrit d'un sombre nuage' (p. 77). Later, when she begins to lose all equanimity, the narrator talks of her 'fougue destructive de la considération qui ne se compose que du calme' (p. 98), and finally we are told of the situation between the lovers: 'Notre vie ne fut qu'un perpétuel orage' (p. 102). Apart from being an aid to psychological presentation, the storm-image contributes to the overall effect of closeness of texture in the work.

6. STRUCTURE

It will perhaps be accepted, on the basis of the remarks of the foregoing pages, that the composition of *Adolphe,* far from offering a loose and episodic development such as might have been expected from Constant's original subtitle to his work *(Anecdote trouvée dans les papiers d'un inconnu),* shows extremely careful attention to the interrelation of detail. In fact the work is anything but anecdotal in its style, and Constant is merely exploiting a well-worn eighteenth-century convention (the chance discovery of an 'authentic' manuscript) as a means of presentation. We are beginning to discover a quite new conception of the novel. The loose linking together of sequences in a linear progression (of which the picaresque novel had been the extreme form) is now being replaced by an approach to the text as an organic totality in which the inner unity dictates the disposition of its elements. In this respect, if one takes a crude historical view, Constant has his rightful place in literary history between Laclos and Flaubert, who both raised the novel to new peaks of perfection while exploiting the prevailing conventions. Having seen something of this approach in the various stylistic devices used by Constant, we should hope to find it again at the level of overall structure. My use of the term 'structure' is intended to cover two aspects: first, the internal mechanisms which motivate the plot; second, the external proportions and divisions of the tale. Let us take these in turn.

It has often been said that Constant's novel has some of the properties of a Racinian drama, with its almost claustrophobic concentration on a central dilemma (for discussion of this see *15*, p. 34 and pp. 43-46). There are, of course, some essential points of difference: Constant's attention to the disappearance of passion rather than its growth, his choice of a prolonged time-scale, the setting of the drama in varied geographical locations, not to mention the preference of a different genre. Of the unities of time and place Constant once wrote:

> [Elles] circonscrivent nos tragédies dans un espace qui en rend la composition difficile, la marche précipitée, l'action fatigante et invraisemblable. Elles contraignent le poète à négliger souvent, dans les événements et les caractères, la vérité de la gradation. (*1*, p. 884)

Yet for all that, the parallel with Racine is a valid one, and is perhaps most evident in Constant's attention to unity of the action.

In addition to all the events in the story being subordinate to the central problem, the tragic incompatibility of the lovers is relentlessly exposed until we reach the final climax. What matters is not the detail of individual developments, but the manner in which each new change intensifies the emotional dilemma. Adolphe's accompaniment of Ellénore to Poland, the recovered inheritance, even the heroine's death – the events in themselves are described with bare simplicity; what interests us in them is their contribution to an overall scheme and the manner in which they combine to produce the total effect. The emphasis is always on the unifying force, never on the constituent elements of the narrative. Even that which comes before the encounter with Ellénore, although in some senses standing apart from the narrative proper, contributes closely to our understanding of the tragic predicament. As in Racinian drama, the problem is present before the introduction of specific circumstances which bring the action into play; and the arrival of Ellénore is the individual element which highlights the complexities of the original matrix.

Unity of action in *Adolphe* is greatly reinforced by the sense of fatality which looms over the story. Most obvious and most immediate among the devices used by Constant is the description of the hero by an outside observer at the outset. Now it is important to stress that, when we see Adolphe through the eyes of the editor, the affair with Ellénore is already in the past and the manuscript already written. It is therefore impossible for the story, when we read it, to have any bearing at all on the fictional present (especially since the editor claims to have delayed ten years before publishing the manuscript). The reader knows and must accept this. Compare such a situation with, for example, that of *Manon Lescaut,* where the Homme de qualité meets Des Grieux for the first time before the latter's departure to America, and then again on his return, at which point the story is recounted. The explanation in *Manon Lescaut* thus finds a natural focal point, which is the journey to America, and it is geared towards a listener who has witnessed some of the earlier events in the story. But the editor in *Adolphe* has not, like his counterpart in *Manon Lescaut,* had any influence on the course of the story; and even his correspondent's claims to have known the participants stand unconfirmed by Adolphe's own account. Nor do we have any real impression that this account is in any way directed towards a specific listener, as is the case in *Manon Lescaut;* indeed, the so-called 'narratee' is, as one critic has pointed out,[12] strangely absent, and only once does Adolphe make an appeal to a second person in his story ('Qui que vous soyez, ne remettez jamais à un autre les intérêts de votre cœur', p. 95). The account is deliberately, almost overbearingly, fixed and static, a characteristic which is reinforced by the presence of the maxims: what took place is not in question, the issue is how and why it took place. As in Racinian tragedy, disaster is known to be inevitable, and the focus shifts to how the human mind may bear with dignity what it is powerless to avoid.

Also in the tragic tradition, Constant is careful to balance inner and outer forces in order to prevent any facile judgement of his hero's guilt or innocence. Adolphe's failures do not in themselves decide the turn of events; the reactions of other people (which he cannot foresee or control) combine with them to produce the tragic outcome. In this respect, Adolphe's avowal of his true sentiments about Ellénore to her friend is something like Phèdre's admission to Œnone of her incestuous passion for Hippolyte, for both confidantes make more active use of the information than had been envisaged by its disclosers. Similarly, the baron de T***'s action in sending Adolphe's letter on to Ellénore shows an outside character taking an unexpected responsibility over feelings which the central character cannot himself fully account for. As Constant suggested in his tribute to Madame de Staël written after her death, it is the artist's duty to suggest the sense of guilt and responsibility, as well as the insidious nature of moral problems, but without pointing the finger of blame in any unequivocal manner:

> Un ouvrage d'imagination ne doit pas avoir un but moral, mais un résultat moral. Il doit ressembler, à cet égard, à la vie humaine qui n'a pas un but, mais qui toujours a un résultat dans lequel la morale trouve nécessairement sa place. (*I*, p. 834)

---

[12] John T. Booker, 'The implied "narrataire" in *Adolphe*', *The French Review*, 51 (1977-78), 666-73.

The most frequent point of comparison to which attention is drawn between Constant's novel and classical tragedy is the particular use he makes of the presence of society. Society represents, either in the form of specific individuals or in the general form of its attitudes, that sense of constraint which is alternately seen either as wholesome discipline or as cruel oppression. Society was, moreover, held by Constant to be something of a modern equivalent to the gods of the ancients, and in one of the most telling remarks he ever penned on the link between his aesthetic and his social beliefs he tells us:

> L'ordre social, l'action de la société sur l'individu, dans les diverses phases et aux diverses époques, ce réseau d'institutions et de conventions qui nous enveloppe dès notre naissance et ne se rompt qu'à notre mort, sont des ressorts tragiques qu'il ne faut que savoir manier. Ils sont tout à fait équivalents à la fatalité des anciens. (*1*, p. 918)

The presence of society, together with the differing responses to its demands on the part of the two lovers, is an important motivating element in the story. Society is most obviously a hostile outer force in the case of Ellénore, bent as it is on her destruction: allowing her a precarious respect before her encounter with Adolphe, expressing its outrage when she abandons all for her lover, treating her as an outcast when she sets up with Adolphe in her father's house. The absolute ascendant of society, which commands total obedience or else exacts dire punishment, is clearly expressed by Adolphe at the beginning of his account when he says: 'Cette société d'ailleurs n'a rien à...craindre. Elle pèse tellement sur nous, son influence sourde est tellement puissante, qu'elle ne tarde pas à nous façonner d'après le moule universel' (p. 40). Herein lies the difference between Adolphe's and Ellénore's attitude, a difference which leads to their inevitable separation. Adolphe, critical of society though he may be, ultimately respects its values and refrains from goading it into anger. If he despises the hypocrisy and

the facility of its judgements, he nevertheless looks to it for
satisfaction of his own ego: his eagerness to earn the respect
of key social figures such as the baron de T***, his yearning
for the pleasure of career satisfaction, his dream of an
acceptable emotional partner, these reveal a conservative
attitude not to be found in the more single-minded Ellénore.
As the novel progresses, the social gap between the lovers
becomes symbolically wider. At first we see them together
in the society of the comte de P***, but later we find them
apart when Adolphe receives an invitation to the house of
the baron de T*** and when Ellénore remains in hiding: she
has become, in the baron de T***'s words, one of those
women 'que l'on ne voit que chez elles' (p. 104). Society
provides a measure by which the two central characters'
development in opposite directions can be gauged. More
than this, it forces the issues by its very presence in their
world; and finally it offers, chorus-like, a running commen-
tary on the actions of the characters – from the range of
reactions displayed when Ellénore leaves the comte de P***,
through the attitude of Adolphe's father who pinpoints the
social implications of his son's behaviour, to the interven-
tions of the baron de T***, and then, all passion spent, to
the two judgements offered at the end of the narrative by the
editor and his correspondent. Society is part of the internal
structure of the novel, and a key element in its equilibrium.

Together with that sense of tragic ambiguity and the
delicate balance of inner and outer forces, the reader may
also be struck by the external proportions of the novel. It
has been said that the ten chapters of this story, taken in
pairs, might be seen as having something of the nature of
the five acts of a tragedy (*24*, pp. 250-54). An alternative
scheme which has been suggested is to see the novel as
falling naturally into three groups of three chapters, with the
tenth and final chapter offering the dénouement (*14*, pp.
303-6). What I should prefer to stress, rather than any
external scheme, is the careful interrelation in the novel of
climaxes of events and climaxes of emotion. These separate
orders are now staggered, now brought together, and the

author's use of such a technique has significant consequences for our reading of the text.

The first part of the novel is marked by one major event,
which is the seduction of Ellénore in the third chapter. The
emotional climax which is the corollary of this event is held
over until the beginning of the fourth chapter: it is the
well-known one-paragraph celebration of love. The simple
technique of delay might not appear in any way unusual (is
it not a conventional means of maintaining interest?) until
we reflect that it could, perhaps, have been more logically
inserted into the narrative in the closing stages of chapter
three, where the narrator is already expressing his joy. As it
stands, it gives the impression of being slightly isolated. It is
known that this paragraph was absent from the 1810 manuscript of *Adolphe* and that it was added for the first edition of
the novel, but does that alone account for the effect of
disjunction? I would prefer to argue that such an effect was
deliberately sought by the author, who wishes to show his
hero's inner life as fragmented in the early stages, or at least
as lacking in continuity. For the introspective young
Adolphe, the real world of cause and effect is at some
distance, and he lives more in the fitful and sporadic
domain of the inner life. As he tells us: 'Je ne demandais
alors qu'à me livrer à ces impressions primitives et fou-
gueuses que jettent l'âme hors de la sphère commune' (pp.
35-36). The relation between the outer and inner world has
not yet been fully established. Ironically, it will come only
in the latter stages of the story.

The interplay between facts and feelings becomes much
more complicated in the middle stages of the novel (i.e. the
rest of chapter four to the end of chapter six). In this section
there are three, or perhaps four, main external events. The
first is Ellénore's departure from the comte de P*** at the
end of chapter four. The second is Adolphe's departure
from D*** to return to his father, half-way through chapter
five. The third – a double event – is the synthesis of the
preceding departures as Adolphe and Ellénore leave together, first for Caden at the end of chapter five, then for
Poland at the end of chapter six (the journey to Poland is, in

terms of the action of the story, a reiteration and a reinforcement rather than an entirely new occurrence). The
symmetry of these departures is itself an eloquent statement
of the anxiety and agitation of the lovers, but into this
scheme Constant injects three emotional climaxes which
maintain the intensity of the drama at an almost unbearable
pitch.

The first of these is the bitter dispute which occurs
between Adolphe and Ellénore half-way through chapter
four, and which prompts the dark diagnosis that 'une
première barrière était franchie. Nous avions prononcé tous
deux des mots irréparables...' (p. 65). The second is Adolphe's act of rebellion against his father and his decision to
remain with Ellénore at the end of chapter five, together
with Ellénore's clear-sighted response ('Vous n'avez que de
la pitié'). The third comes shortly later in chapter six, when
Adolphe makes his own attempt to be forthright ('L'amour
[...] je ne l'ai plus', p. 81). As Alison Fairlie has pointed out
(*17*, p. 226), this moment stands in conspicuous equilibrium
with Ellénore's own moment of truth (moreover, it is one of
the ironies that Adolphe is doing no more than tell her what
she had told him). We find something of the symmetry of
the external action echoed at the level of inner, emotional
high points.

But let us look also to the correlation between external
fact and internal change in these middle chapters. Here we
will find that in two out of three cases an emotional climax
actually precedes the event which will accompany it: the
dispute between Adolphe and Ellénore in chapter four is
followed by Ellénore's separation from the compte de P***;
and Adolphe's revelation to Ellénore in chapter six that he
is no longer in love with her is followed by the departure to
Poland. In both cases, the ordering of the narrative is an
ironic reinforcement of the helplessness of Adolphe's and
Ellénore's situation, for their actions are carried out at a
time when irreparable damage has already been done. Only
once in the middle section of the novel do external and
internal events coincide, and this is when Ellénore accuses
Adolphe of experiencing no more than pity at the moment

when the lovers are departing for Caden. Appropriately, this occurs at the precise mid-way point of the novel, and Ellénore's insight is given a privileged status amidst the surrounding confusion. It is the first occasion when an event immediately elicits an adjacent emotional response.

In the latter stages of the story (chapters seven to ten) there is an apparent return to the pattern of its early stages, with emotional climaxes following on from external actions. The difference is that the delay no longer appears as a process of disjunction, but rather as the temporal progression of cause and effect. It is as though the memory of Ellénore's insight has jolted the narrator, who now gradually emerges from the confusion and begins to perceive a coherent pattern in his past conduct. There are three points at which we see this. The first is in chapter seven, where the significant first encounter with the baron de T*** prompts a new moment of inner intensity as Adolphe wanders alone at night. The second is in chapter eight where two external events – the intercession of Ellénore's friend, and Ellénore's invitation of local people into her house – have their backlash in the scenes of frenzied conflict between the lovers described in the final paragraph of the chapter. And the third, perhaps most obviously, is the baron de T***'s action to separate the couple (chapter nine) followed by Ellénore's emotional delirium at the beginning of the final chapter as she falls into fatal sickness.

This device of separation and intertwining of the external and internal high points in the novel has considerable advantages in a text of such small proportions. It creates, through its pattern of intermittences and echoes, the impression of density and depth; and with great economy of means, the author is able to scatter the moments of tension more evenly and more widely. But the overall distribution tells us something else. At first, for the inexperienced and introverted young hero, the world of emotions and the world of real events are unsynchronized and separate; in the confused middle stages of his relationship they seem even to be of two different orders altogether. But they are forced together in the middle of the novel with Ellénore's insight, and thereafter an overall pattern of cause and effect begins to emerge. Whilst Adolphe's explicit account of his relation-ship with Ellénore stresses its progression towards increasing disorder, the underlying structure of that account shows the gradual emergence of order. This is an irony which rein-forces Constant's deliberately ambivalent presentation of his hero.

The careful and controlled structuring of the novel is confirmed again by the move to the epistolary level with which it is concluded. Although an apparent sop to an eighteenth-century convention, Constant's use of the two letters of judgement by way of epilogue is an amplification of what is already present within the narrative: the turning of Adolphe's judgements against him, and the alternative in-terpretations of events which are to be found in the extracts given from other people's letters (the two trends coming together in the final pages of the story, where Ellénore's letter provides the transition to the external point of view). It is perhaps of interest to note that the 1810 manuscript of *Adolphe* did not contain the concluding letters, and that the *Avis de l'éditeur* correspondingly offered different reasons for the publication of the manuscript (this, we are told, was found together with some diamonds, and it is in the hope of returning them to their rightful owner that the editor is having the story printed).[13] The manifest superiority of the reworked ending comes of its being structurally an integral part of the work. The earlier convention, which often implied that literary merit was the very last reason for publication, is now turned upside down by Constant. He is using it in order to complete the effect of unity for which he strives.[14] But there is a further aspect of the epistolary conclusion which merits a moment's attention, for it also exploits another fascinating undercurrent in the novel.

---

[13] For the text of the variant in the original *Avis* see *4,* p. 15.

[14] For a full discussion of this aspect of the novel see Alison Fairlie, 'Framework as a suggestive art in Constant's *Adolphe* (with remarks on its relation to Chateaubriand's *René)*', *Australian Journal of French Studies,* Special Number, 16, pts. 1-2 (1979), 6-16.

That undercurrent – which has implications on the whole way in which we look at the structure of the work – is the existence of letters and documents which the reader never gets to see. In his reply to the editor, the correspondent refers to a series of letters which he is sending and which, he says, will give some insight into what later happened to Adolphe. The editor himself replies, after reading these letters, that he could have guessed at the continued misery of Adolphe's existence even had he not received this further information. What we have here is a text or a series of texts, known to the characters and discussed by them, but quite unknowable to the reader. This is an ironic inversion of what so often happens in the epistolary novel, where the reader holds documents unknown to at least some of the characters. Now these letters and documents referred to at the end of the story are far from being the only source of alternative information which is mentioned. What they do is increase our sense of the possible extensions in different directions of Adolphe's account: whether it be in Ellénore's direction, in the series of documents and personal papers which she leaves after her death, or in her correspondence with Adolphe when the latter is at his father's house; or in the comte de P***'s direction, for we know that he writes to Ellénore while she is away in chapter two, and that he writes to her again later offering her half of his recovered fortune; or in the direction of Adolphe's father, for we read but fragments of the correspondence between him and his son, and we know also that he corresponds with the baron de T***. Of the innumerable documents, letters, conversations, reminiscences and interpretations, the final account has been wrested in all its incompleteness. We are aware of the difference and the potential conflict between Adolphe's own version and the other possible versions of the story.

For all its classical structure and elegant proportions there is, then, a deliberate air of asymmetry about *Adolphe*. The directness of its line of action, the careful patterning of its themes and images, the totality of effect created by the organization of the text, are undercut by our awareness that we are in possession of a limited segment of the story, the incompleteness of which is epitomized by the final withholding of extra information about the hero. Beneath the unified surface of the text we discern gaps, additions and alterations, and our attention is drawn to the fact that the process of converting lived experience into written form is by no means the monopoly of the narrating Adolphe. The continued mention within his own account of other written documents underlines that others are doing precisely the same as he, and the only reason that his own story happens to have a privileged status is because it is the only one we possess. We are not therefore left with the impression (as we may be, say, in classical theatre) that we have a perfect and unalterable representation of an action. The work is lacunary in its very conception, posing the problem of how reality can be perceived through words and thus evoking a theme which will be a major concern of modern writers.

Just as we are in the end obliged to judge Constant's style by a standard other than that of formal completeness, so too we must look in his presentation of character for something other than well-proportioned exemplars of human psychology or morality. Although presented in the light of specific themes, Constant's characters are distinguished above all by their personal responses to given situations. Through them, the author's view of the world comes to life in individual ways, and through them the general and the particular are fused.

Part Two

Presentation of Character

1. Background

In a comparison of French and German approaches to characterization in drama, Constant once wrote:

> Les Allemands n'écartent [du caractère] de leurs personnages rien de ce qui constituait leur individualité; ils nous les présentent avec leurs faiblesses, leurs inconséquences, et cette mobilité ondoyante qui appartient à la nature humaine et qui forme les êtres réels. (*1,* pp. 868-69)

Within the taut economy of a narrative such as *Adolphe*, one cannot expect to find the leisurely development of character which Constant admired in German drama. Yet critics have in the past often hastily concluded that, apart from the hero himself, there were no real characters in the novel: Ellénore, especially, was seen either as a shadowy foil to the narrator or as a lifeless synthesis of women whom Constant himself had known. The balance has been rectified by criticism of the last two decades, which has pointed out Constant's sureness of touch and his alertness to what is most revealing even in minor figures (see in particular Alison Fairlie's study of character, *16*). If the small canvas of *Adolphe* forbids the broad sweep of the brush, there is on the other hand a selective attention to details which highlight hidden assumptions or conflicts in individual behaviour. It is a suggestive rather than an extensive approach, but it leads by another route to that impression of 'mobilité ondoyante' which Constant saw as the essential goal of character portrayal.

The effect of a substantial and varied picture of human behaviour is created even in Constant's adumbrations of background social groups. These are evoked at several points in the novel. There is the court society of the town of D***, and the social circle into which the comte de P*** introduces Adolphe; then there is the concentrated description of reactions within these groups to Ellénore's separation from the count. Later, when Adolphe leaves D*** to return home, his father's own entourage is briefly sketched, and later still we see the baron de T***'s friends and the contacts invited by Ellénore into her father's house; finally, there is the clerical gathering of the closing chapter. Let us, by way of example, look at two descriptions of the background group in the early chapters.

The first is of the court society in D***. Here, the general picture is given in a few swift strokes: the obscure prince sees himself as protector of 'les hommes éclairés' who take up residence in the town, but the fact that an unremarkable figure such as the young Adolphe should be seen as something of a novelty and a curiosity suggests the boredom which reigns in the group as a whole (pp. 38-39). Then, as Adolphe begins by his persiflage to display contempt for these people, the focus sharpens: recipients of his confidences are unsettled by this ambiguous sign of intimacy; doubts arise over his character and he is labelled, by those who take comfort in generalizations, as ill-willed or spiteful. Further life is added when there is a moment's concentration on an individual within the group whose attitude to Adolphe is somewhat different: this is the young friend who, after a long and difficult struggle, succeeds in a love affair. The friend's spontaneous verbalization of his feelings, both in adversity and in triumph, is rapidly pinpointed: 'Comme il ne m'avait point caché ses revers et ses peines, il se crut obligé de me communiquer ses succès: rien n'égalait ses transports et l'excès de sa joie' (p. 42). The careful inclusion of the words 'il se crut obligé' enhances the power of this little sketch, where we sense that the narrator might well have been an unenthusiastic listener and the friend imprudently garrulous.

My second example of a background social description comes at the beginning of chapter five, when Ellénore has left the comte de P***. Here, in the course of a few concentrated paragraphs, Constant gives a particularly vivid and varied account of attitudes and reactions within a group. There is, to start with, the hypocritical moralizing which fails to give Ellénore any credit for her past fidelity; there is the shallow and affected horror at her abandonment of her children; and the self-righteous claim by other women that the whole of their sex is tarnished by her example. And there are the individual reactions towards her: the comte de P***'s two female relatives, whose spitefulness has long been seeking an excuse to unleash itself; or the men who now seek out Ellénore's company because, as they say, they have always known her, or because she is still beautiful, or because they seriously reckon on their chances of success; and finally there is the man who, after ill-judged advances, resorts to verbal vilification and provokes Adolphe to a duel. At the same time, reactions to Adolphe himself are no less suggestively portrayed: friends of his father who are present in this circle pronounce judgement, others drop hints loaded with reproach, and others go even wider of the mark by congratulating him fatuously on his success. Into the general picture of a society alert to what is unconventional or scandalous within its ranks, Constant thus succeeds in injecting a range of specific and telling examples. Yet he never loses sight, despite this rich description, of his main subject, which is Adolphe's own profound feeling of uneasiness.

Standing out against the social backcloth of Constant's novel, there are two minor sketches which illustrate his ability to give that vital touch of reality to characters whose role is only marginal. The first of these is the old lady whose conversations with the narrator are evoked at the beginning, and the second is the friend of Ellénore to whom Adolphe confides the true state of his feelings.

The foremost quality of the old lady lies in what the narrator describes as her 'grande force d'âme' (p. 37). Relentlessly and doggedly refusing to submit to society's dic-

tates, she sacrifices both hope and pleasure and falls back
on her inner intellectual resources. Her youthful enthusiasm, undiminished by the passing of time, reveals itself in
the 'conversations inépuisables' (p. 38) with the young
Adolphe. The character of Ellénore's friend, on the other
hand, could not be more different. Whilst there is no clear
proof that this emissary between the lovers acts out of
self-interest, there is here a suggestion at least that we are in
the presence of a hopeful rival for Adolphe's affections. As
the latter tells us: 'La femme qui m'écoutait fut émue de
mon récit: elle vit de la générosité dans ce que j'appelais de
la faiblesse, du malheur dans ce que j'appelais de la dureté'
(p. 95). Is there something beyond the call of duty in that
emotion she shows on listening to Adolphe? And is it
prudent, given her status as Ellénore's friend, to put quite
such a flattering interpretation on Adolphe's behaviour?
Certainly, Ellénore's subsequent reaction towards this
friend, and her sarcastic remark about 'le zèle de certaines
amitiés' (p. 96), suggest that she for one has not been duped.
Thus we are alerted to the manifold possibilities of what is
no more than a miniature sketch of an incompetent go-
between. But, having quickened our curiosity, Constant
wisely leaves it unsatisfied, since that is a surer means of
retaining it.

2.   SECONDARY CHARACTERS

Beyond the portrayal of social groups and of figures
whom Constant briefly sketches into his narrative, we come
to the fuller depiction of individuals who are present at
various stages in the story, and whose own character is
instrumental in its unfolding.

The first of these is Adolphe's father, incisively charac-
terized as a highly sensitive, even volatile nature, yet who
adopts in his habitual social intercourse either an icy mask
or an air of rakish detachment. In the first portrait of the
father we see the split personality, able to give full expression to itself in letters, yet unable to sustain the stress of

direct human contact (pp. 35-36). This impression will be confirmed later in the story. In the one scene where Adolphe and his father are in each other's presence, the latter makes a few staccato remarks before speech fails him altogether and he leaves the room. How different is the behaviour of Adolphe's father from the easy, urbane manner of his friend the baron de T***. How lacking in strategy is this reaction to his son's liaison with Ellénore. And how devoid of those mellifluous tones of the baron de T***'s speech is his own, where choking impotence deprives him of the ability to link his thoughts: 'On m'assure que l'ancienne maîtresse du comte de P*** est dans cette ville. Je vous ai toujours laissé une grande liberté...' (p. 76). The clumsy threefold movement of conjunctions in the latter part of this same speech ('*et* je n'ai jamais rien voulu savoir...; *mais* il ne vous convient pas...; *et* je vous avertis...') increases the effect of disjointedness, and reinforces the impression that this man is helpless in face-to-face situations.

In the letters he will write to Adolphe, however, the father will appear quite differently. Here he is in control of himself and able to express and follow through his thoughts. The order and balance of his sentences will offer a striking contrast to his spoken style. This is shown in the letter Adolphe receives at the beginning of chapter six, when he has eloped with Ellénore: 'Vous avez vingt-quatre ans', writes the father, bringing to the forefront the problem of the age of majority (which was twenty-five). Then come three statements of intention, all with the first-person pronoun and future tense: 'Je n'exercerai pas contre vous une autorité qui touche à son terme...' (providing the link with the opening statement); 'je cacherai même...votre étrange démarche' (moving on to Adolphe's own conduct and adding emphasis with the adverb); and finally 'je répandrai le bruit que vous êtes parti par mes ordres' (building on the implications of the two preceding statements). In the second half of the letter, he switches from 'je' to 'vous': 'Vous sentirez vous-même...'; 'Votre naissance, vos talents, votre fortune...'; 'Votre lettre...'; 'Vous consumez...'. This move from first to second person is a planned part of the father's rhetoric, as he moves towards a more active (and guilt-provoking) assessment of his son's behaviour. And this time his language will have the effect that later the baron de T***'s words will have. Adolphe writes that 'la lettre de mon père me perça de mille coups de poignard' (pp. 78-79).

If the father's varying success at communication is due in part to the situation in which he finds himself (spoken or written), it might also be attributed to a change of attitude. In the early stages he emerges as a figure who, either through weakness or over-sensitivity, manifestly fails to live up to his responsibilities. Until confronted with the results of his cynical attitude towards women, he is perhaps not greatly concerned about the real issues. But as he becomes more aware of what he sees as his son's aberration, there enters into his reaction an element of regret and remorse which is quite at odds with the glib humour of the early stages. There is already some sharpness in his mention of 'une autorité qui touche à son terme', and even bitterness in the letter we read at the beginning of chapter seven when he talks of 'l'indépendance que vous avez toujours su défendre avec succès contre votre père' (p. 86). But there is, beyond this, a hint of a belatedly emerging awareness of responsibility. This letter from Adolphe's father seems to reveal a quite different degree of commitment from that of the man who, in the early stages of the novel, had shown such indulgence towards his son's misdemeanours. He is now eager to point out the significance of his son's behaviour, and moreover pinpoints the key change in the relationship between Adolphe and Ellénore now that they have arrived in Poland: 'Ce n'est plus vous qui la protégez, c'est elle qui vous protège'. The tone has become firmer, the judgement blunter; and Adolphe's father is obviously quite aware of his son's sensitivity to the stark formulation in words of a moral problem. This is a considerable move forward from the easygoing attitude of the opening pages where, for example, a prolongation of Adolphe's stay in D*** was granted apparently without a second thought. Adolphe's father is now actively trying to influence the course of

events, and he will continue to do so through the interme-
diary of the baron de T***, who acts on his behalf when he
is no longer present in person.

Foremost among the minor portraits of the first half of
the novel is that of the comte de P***. Most striking about
this character, whose function is to represent the dispos-
sessed aristocracy and to serve as the robbed lover, is
Constant's refusal to make of him a villain. Certainly, there
are failures on his part – his lack of awareness of Ellénore's
true feelings and needs, his attitude of superiority towards
her, his vindictive offer of half his fortune on condition that
she leave Adolphe – but these, far from making a caricature
of him, serve to render him more human and more compre-
hensible.

Initially the count appears as the urbane and affable
society man, of somewhat the same slant as Adolphe's
father and the baron de T*** (it is pointed out by Adolphe
that his acquaintance with the comte de P*** is made
through family connections). The count clearly enjoys the
social esteem in which he is held, and will use it to his
advantage. He is concerned that Ellénore should be respect-
ed within his own circle, and is sufficiently influential to be
able to impose silence on any murmurings of dissent. He is
the natural leader of his group, both by status and by
character. His goal in life is a concrete one: the recovery of
his fortune, and thereby his full social rank. He expects
Ellénore to be equally committed to this goal, and feelings
which are not in some way directed towards it are, as far as
he is concerned, irrelevant. The anarchy of the inner life
does not, in the early stages, enter into his view of the world.

When Ellénore returns after her first absence, the count
is intent to turn her arrival into a social occasion. The real
reason for her absence seems quite genuinely to be beyond
his comprehension. His first assumption had been that his
command to her to return would automatically be obeyed
('Je vais lui écrire: elle reviendra sûrement dans quelques
jours'), and the fact that 'son retour fut moins prompt que
ne l'espérait le comte de P***' (p. 49) was scarcely enough

to raise the alarm in him. Concerned to play the role of good host as he leads Adolphe to Ellénore, he further reveals his failure to grasp the situation when he describes the young man to his future mistress (somewhat unfortunately) as 'l'un des hommes que votre départ inattendu a le plus étonnés' (p. 51). Now another writer might have made something very different of this situation; but the irony which is present throughout the episode is never allowed to degenerate into mockery, and although we have information which the count does not, it is not at the expense of his dignity. There is nothing underhand in his manner, and to say, for example, that he is trying to hurt Ellénore by insisting publicly on her 'départ inattendu' would, I think, be taking things too far.

It is only after Ellénore has been seduced by Adolphe that the count suffers a loss of dignity. In the brief moments when we now glimpse him, he appears as a very different figure, wounded and on the defensive. 'Il me reçut chaque jour d'un air plus froid et plus sombre', Adolphe tells us (p. 63). His attitude emerges vividly in the small scene where he, Adolphe, Ellénore and the children are all together in a room. Astonishment is on the children's faces, and the silence weighs heavy. The count reacts with sharpness, as he hints to Adolphe that he ought to be thinking of his career, adding provocatively for Ellénore's benefit: 'Tout le monde peut-être ne pense pas ici comme moi' (p. 64). The clumsy yet stinging remark seems loaded with his own hurt pride. But acrimony is later replaced by authoritarianism when he forbids Ellénore to invite Adolphe into the house again; and there is desperation in his futile final act, when he offers half his fortune to Ellénore on condition that she abandon Adolphe.

It is clear that the count loses his self-assurance after the seduction of Ellénore. The resultant transformation in his behaviour is no doubt attributable in part to his frustration at being confronted with the results of his past attitude towards her. Not only had he failed to appreciate his mistress's real needs, but he had also been content to use her. There was, indeed, an all too suspect symmetry between Ellénore's situation as a mother but not a wife and the count's own situation as an aristocrat by title but not by wealth: both were in some way deprived of their 'rightful' status. 'Il peut se passer de moi maintenant', says Ellénore when she knows that the count is on the point of recovering his fortune (p. 66). Is it because she knows that the count, once restored to his full rank, will no longer wish to associate with a woman of ambiguous station? Was the end of the liaison between Ellénore and the count perhaps in sight notwithstanding the presence of Adolphe? Is the count's pique due in part to his having been pre-empted in the matter? Such issues are, in the end, left open. What does emerge with certainty, however, is that while the count suffers genuinely from the departure of Ellénore, his failure to understand her persists. The ultimate offer of half of his fortune is, to a character such as her, something of an insult. We must imagine either that he knows she will refuse and wishes merely to score a cheap point, or that his knowledge of her character is so scant that he cannot foresee her reaction. Either way, this represents a pathetic failure of communication and shows a final loss of dignity on the part of the comte de P***. It is a convincing last touch to his development.

There is no such dramatic development in the chief minor study of the second half of the novel, the baron de T***. Rather, in the case of such a character, it is appropriate that there should be no change of course, for the man is complete, equal to the challenges he is faced with, and never confronted by a real personal dilemma. We are here in the presence of an old man whose turbulent years are well behind him, and who can look upon the troubles of others with benign and avuncular detachment. As Adolphe puts it, he is 'un vieux ministre dont l'âme était usée, et qui se rappelait vaguement que, dans sa jeunesse, il avait aussi été tourmenté par des histoires d'amour' (p. 104). [15]

---

[15] For a study of the baron de T*** which both stresses the importance of his role and emphasizes the coherence of his character, see *16*, pp. 261-62.

There are some similarities and some sharp contrasts between the baron de T*** and his earlier counterpart the comte de P***. Both are important figureheads in small social groups, and within those circles they freely use their power and their charm; the comte de P*** is for Adolphe a family contact, and the baron de T*** a personal friend of his father's; they both welcome Adolphe into their groups. But the comte de P*** is a younger man (he is described by Adolphe in his first mention of him as an 'homme de quarante ans') and shows himself to be vulnerable, whereas the baron de T*** is self-assured to the point of ruthlessness. In addition to this, the baron has a skill which the comte de P*** entirely lacks – the ability to see through and judge other characters. And whereas the comte de P*** is prepared to repress inner sentiment for the purpose of social gain (until sentiment can be repressed no longer), the baron de T*** does not need to repress any feelings, because he simply does not experience their tyranny.

The baron is thus in a position to be far more open and direct with Adolphe than could the comte de P***, and the incisive manner of his first remarks on the subject of Ellénore (pp. 87-88) reveals at once a tactical awareness which might be expected of a career diplomat, a concern for both Adolphe and the latter's father, and an ability to come to a clear decision on the complex moral problems with which Adolphe is grappling. In this strength lies also the baron's limitation. For all his percipience, he will ultimately misjudge the effect which his intervention will have: this is because his opinion is dictated by what he sees as the overriding need to detach Adolphe from Ellénore. His opinion about Ellénore is therefore simplistic, and his predictions about her wrong. As he tells Adolphe on their first meeting: 'Il n'y a pas une de ces femmes passionnées dont le monde est plein qui n'ait protesté qu'on la ferait mourir en l'abandonnant; il n'y en a pas une qui ne soit encore en vie et qui ne soit consolée' (p. 87). Now this particular argument (wrapped up, of course, as worldly knowledge) may not ultimately weigh very strongly in Adolphe's decision to leave Ellénore: but it is clear that the baron himself believes it. He is not sensitive towards Ellénore, certainly never meets her, and sees her purely as the woman of tarnished reputation. This attitude will remain unchanged when, later, the baron invites Adolphe to a reception at his house. Telling him that he will meet 'les plus jolies femmes de Pologne', he adds somewhat riskily: 'Vous n'y trouverez pas, il est vrai, celle que vous aimez; j'en suis fâché, mais il y a des femmes que l'on ne voit que chez elles' (p. 104). This is clearly near the limit of what the baron can get away with. He has already frightened Adolphe off on one occasion, but he knows that if the young man does fail to leap to his mistress's defence, then another small victory will have been won against him; and this is exactly what happens. The baron de T***'s calculations demand that he take such risks, and that he shed the most unflattering light on Ellénore.

But the risk of offence run by the baron de T*** is only one tactic among many in his small war of attrition. It is in the variety of his behaviour that he comes to life. From being ruthless and upsetting, he becomes caressing and cajoling, as he talks to the young man of his career and explains that he has heard of his promise and ability; or he plays the card of disinterestedness when, on writing to Adolphe after the latter's absence, he says that the liaison with Ellénore is secondary to the fact that Adolphe is the son of a dear friend; or again, he encourages Adolphe's small successes within his own social entourage and gives him duties relating to his ministerial office. Then he allows Adolphe to feel the acute pain of embarrassment when, on the evening of the reception, the latter hears whispers about his situation; having manipulated the young man into this corner, the baron then comes to the rescue and helps him to earn the respect and the esteem of the other guests. Later still, when Adolphe is unable to make a firm decision for himself, the baron acts on his behalf, sending the fateful letter on to Ellénore together with a letter of his own.

The baron's tactics, in all their variety, are governed throughout by the single-minded aim of separating Adolphe and Ellénore. It might, of course, seem that he relegates

moral problems to a position of secondary importance
behind effective action, and that he thereby emerges as
blunt and insensitive. But his answer to this would be that
his action is its own justification. For him, the real moral
issue is the rescue of a friend's son from damaging circumstances, and he can therefore claim (as indeed he does) to be
acting out of loyalty. As well as being a convincingly
portrayed figure, the baron de T*** thus provides us with
yet another angle on the moral issues in the novel.

3. ELLÉNORE

The masterpiece of characterization in Constant's work
is undoubtedly the figure of Ellénore. Whilst the question of
real-life sources of the heroine has in the past diverted much
scholarly energy, recent criticism has looked more closely to
the inner coherence of the character, and its judgement has
been almost unanimously favourable. One critic has even
attempted a rewriting of the story from Ellénore's point of
view, and offers in the same volume the most extensive
account to date of her character *(18)*. But the landmark, as
far as Constant's heroine is concerned, is still the short
analysis by Alison Fairlie *(16,* pp. 254-60). She points out
that Adolphe's particular quality of sensitivity towards the
suffering of others allows a degree of focus rare in a
first-person novel, and that, far from being a patchwork of
real reminiscences on the part of the author, Ellénore is a
convincing and coherent character whose development is
influenced on three levels: her basic nature as a woman, her
particular social position, and her individual temperament
(with its key qualities of 'dévouement' and 'fierté'). I do not
propose, in the following pages, to go over this ground again
and attempt a complete portrait of Ellénore. What I should
like to do is focus on her individual temperament and see
how the development of character is generated by inner
tensions.

What seems fundamental to the character of Ellénore
from the moment when Adolphe first describes her (pp. 43-45)

is the presence of deep internal conflict. This manifests itself immediately in a series of antithetical tendencies, where she seems at odds with the circumstances of her own life, or as Constant puts it, 'en lutte constante avec sa destinée'. Despite a 'situation désavantageuse' (a disturbed family past is referred to) she has shown distinction of character; despite the apparent differences of character and station between herself and the comte de P***, their relationship has survived on the basis of her devotion; despite her no more than average intelligence, Ellénore's ideas have freshness and charm; despite the irregularity of her own conduct, she adheres rigidly to the precepts of conventional morality. But that secret turmoil also manifests itself in Ellénore's restless behaviour: with her children she will be in turn intensely affectionate or unnaturally constrained; in social situations her mood will veer between taciturn reverie and excited volubility. There seems to be no 'point of rest' in Ellénore's character, pulled as it is in opposite directions. The corollary of this is that, when there is a change in her circumstances, the precarious balance will inevitably be upset and the character turn to extremes. It is not surprising that Ellénore shows fear of change both before her liaison with Adolphe and during its early stages. She knows that it is in her nature to over-react. Her solution, with the comte de P***, has been to repress her inner vitality, albeit at the cost of serenity. When finally she focuses that vitality on Adolphe, the accumulation of past pains makes normal, healthy self-expression virtually impossible. This, in conjunction with her age and social situation, means that the dice are firmly loaded against her relationship with Adolphe.

In the 1810 manuscript of his novel Constant had, in the initial portrait of Ellénore, included an explicit reference to her past before describing her liaison with the comte de P***: 'Ellénore, c'était son nom, soit imprudence, soit passion, soit malheur de circonstances, avait eu, dans un âge fort tendre, une aventure d'éclat, dont les détails me sont restés inconnus' (see variant, p. 277). It was after one of Constant's London readings of his manuscript that a friend,

Lady Campbell, advised exclusion of these lines, and they
were duly omitted from the 1816 edition. The result of the
change is of great significance to our understanding of
the character of Ellénore. No longer are we led to conclude
she had formed her relationship with the comte de P*** as a
means of escaping a scandalous past. What emerges from
the definitive version is quite different: it is the suggestion
that, whatever may have been the circumstances surrounding the beginning of Ellénore's liaison with the count, her
devotion to him is a free choice and even an inner need.
The channelling of her energy towards the recovery of the
count's fortune is not purely a result of the particular
conditions which bring the couple together. There is in
Ellénore a desire to keep the lid firmly closed on an agitated
inner life, and this seems to be her response to a much more
fundamental sense of personal anarchy.

It is of course obvious that Ellénore's relationship with
the comte de P*** is unsatisfactory, and that he is using her
both materially and psychologically. His condescension towards her automatically excludes equality from their relationship, and it places a taboo on the expression of inner
feelings. But has it been sufficiently appreciated that, by the
normal pattern of inversion, Ellénore is probably also using
the count? After all, here is a man who expects and even
welcomes the 'dévouement' which is essential to Ellénore –
without questioning its motives, as Adolphe will do later.
This provides her with the perfect cover-up, and the relationship with the count thus emerges less as an unwelcome
burden forced upon Ellénore by adverse circumstances than
as a powerful self-imposed constraint, the origins of which
we cannot know. But the effect of Ellénore's 'dévouement' is
to create conflict between her notion of duty and her desire
for freedom. It follows that when this conflict is initially
resolved in her relationship with Adolphe it will subsequently, through sheer force of habit, seek other means of
reasserting itself.

The great changes which take place in Ellénore once she
has been seduced by Adolphe – that relinquishing of all
sense of shame, the readiness to risk all, the sudden and

total focusing of all her energy on her lover – result in a euphoric release of emotions which, for so long, had been held rigidly in check. Ellénore now finds herself in unknown territory, where outer constraint no longer exists and where inner freedom is no longer circumscribed by obstacles ('Ellénore n'avait jamais été aimée de la sorte', says Adolphe, p. 58). But it is one of the ironies of the story that Adolphe will soon prove to be as incapable of responding to the intense and vital inner Ellénore as was the comte de P***. The pattern, naturally, is very different in each case: whereas the comte de P*** prevented the very expression of Ellénore's feelings by his coldness, Adolphe initially encourages them, only to discover that he cannot bear the intensity of focus on himself. The result, for Ellénore, will be that she wavers in her newly found freedom, then re-enacts what she already knows by way of attempting to recover her equilibrium. The wish for constraint, for so long a part of her world before being pushed brutally aside on the arrival of Adolphe, returns in more circuitous ways.

As the relationship develops and Ellénore becomes increasingly aware of Adolphe's inability to respond to her, she will take society's accusations more to heart. This is a means of looking for limitations to her freedom, of reassuring herself that the 'old order' still stands. The appeal to social constraint may take several forms. It can appear as a sense of the sacrifices she has made, as when she accuses Adolphe, during their first dispute, 'de l'avoir remise, aux yeux du public, dans la situation équivoque dont elle avait cherché toute sa vie à sortir' (p. 65); or it may masquerade as a rebellion against the unfair judgements of society, as when she points out on leaving the count: 'J'ai rempli pendant dix ans mes devoirs mieux qu'aucune femme, et cette opinion ne m'en a pas moins repoussée du rang que je méritais' (p. 66); or again, it may take the form of a refusal of the material advantages offered by society, as when Ellénore turns down the chance of half the count's fortune. The fact that her attitude towards society is often one of revolt does not in any way diminish her sense of its power: rather, it seems that she is thereby seeking a reminder that there are parameters to her freedom, and this gives at least the echo of a feeling of security. At the same time it forces her to direct her attention more exclusively towards Adolphe, and thus nurtures the love on which she has staked everything.

However, Ellénore's moody awareness of the disapproval of society leads into a vicious circle: the more she feels shunned, the more exclusive is her attachment to her lover; and the more exclusive her attachment, the more she feels shunned. Constant points out in his prefaces to the novel the dangers to women of exclusive relationships such as these, and the theme is also developed in a passage of the *Lettre sur Julie*. That passage is worth quoting since it gives an insight into the dilemma with which Ellénore tries unsuccessfully to cope:

> Ce n'est qu'à l'époque de ce qu'on a nommé leur défaite, que les femmes commencent à avoir un but précis, celui de conserver l'amant pour lequel elles ont fait ce qui doit leur sembler un grand sacrifice. Les hommes, au contraire, à cette même époque, cessent d'avoir un but: ce qui en était un pour eux devient un lien. (*1*, pp. 810-11)

The passage finds many an echo in *Adolphe*, both in the vocabulary it uses and in the ideas it expresses. Ellénore finds that instead of being precariously divided between 'dévouement' to a social ideal (the count's recovery of his fortune) and her own inner volatility, she has nothing but her private feelings to live for. That those feelings should assume weird proportions, like fungi in the dark, is an inevitable consequence. As the relationship develops and her stress is prolonged, she increasingly has outbursts of anger: there is that first moment in chapter four when she accuses Adolphe of being unenthusiastic about the continuation of his stay in D***; then the three-hour scene when she seeks him out in his home town; and finally the 'perpétuel orage' of life in Poland (p. 102).

Alternating with, and counterbalancing, those moments of passionate rage, there is another, quieter side to Ellénore's character which will ultimately earn her the reader's admiration rather than mere pity. This is the element of weary and sometimes desperate lucidity which returns throughout, and which in the moments leading up to her death gives her at least a glimpse of serenity. Volatile though she may be, Ellénore is far from being blinded by her love for Adolphe. The latter may imagine, when he returns to his father's house, that the letters he writes to Ellénore are sufficient to deceive her ('j'en disais toujours assez pour l'abuser', p. 73); but Ellénore is much more perceptive, and when later she rejects the idea of going to Poland on her own, one of her arguments is that the letters of Adolphe would be hurtfully cold (p. 83). She also knows, almost throughout their liaison, that Adolphe is not in love with her. The early assessment that 'Vous n'avez que de la pitié' (p. 78) is followed by a number of other clear and realistic insights. On the occasion of her refusal to depart for Poland, she points out that her sacrifices have not elicited from Adolphe the response she might have hoped for: 'Je n'ai pas la consolation de me dire que, par le sacrifice de toute ma vie, je sois parvenue à vous inspirer le sentiment que je méritais' (p. 83). Later, if she asks a friend to intercede between herself and Adolphe, this is because she knows that there are things which her lover cannot tell her directly: far from being insensitive and domineering, she is showing proof of clear-headedness, and the failure of her calculations is due principally to circumstances beyond her control. She will, of course, be misled from time to time by false insights, such as when she imagines that her flirting with other men is having the desired effect on Adolphe; but she does not wilfully ignore the evidence for long, and even on this occasion Adolphe tells us that 'elle s'alarmait de ne me voir aucune inquiétude' (p. 100).

But it is in the final view we have of Ellénore – in the moments preceding her death and in the letter which we see afterwards – that we have the greatest proofs of her lucidity. As she approaches her death, she recognizes that there is no point in building false hopes once more; and when Adolphe renews his protestations of love she responds by pointing

out its impossibility. As she tells him: 'L'amour était toute
ma vie. Il ne pouvait être la vôtre' (p. 111). In her last
moments she is thus able to put accusation and blame aside,
by accepting the principle that love between herself and
Adolphe was impossible. The letter to Adolphe may not
have this breadth of perspective (it was of course written
well before this scene) but it too reveals an ability to analyse
and assess the relationship with honest precision, and in
it Ellénore gives her view without any of the self-
aggrandizement which occasionally characterizes Adolphe's
language. Without bitterness, she also predicts the loneliness
which Adolphe is to suffer after her death – proof of which
we have by this time already received. That this passionate
woman is also capable of such detachment seems to be the
final touch on Constant's part in bringing her character
alive.

The presence of such conflicting qualities in Ellénore as
volatility, weary lucidity and the degree of serenity which
seems to be achieved against the very grain of her own
character, might prompt some readers to judge her uncon-
vincing. But the particular opposites which come together
in her character are coherently linked: her fiery temperament is consonant with the lucidity she shows, precisely
because each is a reaction against the other; and her lucidity, by concentrating on what is positive, leads on to the
detachment of the end. It is through conflict that Ellénore
comes to life, and through conflict that she evolves. But
what is noteworthy, in this novel of ambivalence, is that she
finally sees beyond the conflict and glimpses the wholeness which for so long had evaded her. She offers a message
of hope in what is sometimes seen as a novel of despair.

4. ADOLPHE

i. The problem of distinguishing characteristics. It is in
the very nature of first-person narration that the main
character cannot have the same clarity of outline as the
secondary characters. Whereas it is part of his task to

impose unity and coherence on others, offering us a series of constructs by which to judge them, his own character is more likely to emerge as fragmentary. His is the eye which beholds everything but itself. Usually we do not have the distance necessary to judge or even perceive him clearly. If he is not frequently seen and assessed by others within the text, he may appear as shadowy and unreal.

Now it must be conceded that, in the case of Adolphe, we do have a significant number of outside views: first the editor's, when he meets the hero at the Italian inn; later, when the story ends, the moral judgements pronounced by both the editor and his correspondent; to say nothing of those points in the story where the focus is shifted and Adolphe finds himself being judged by others (most notably by his father, Ellénore and the baron de T***). Our first question must, then, be to ask what it is possible to know about Adolphe on the basis of such judgements, before looking to his own inner world for corroboration or qualification of them.

The moral judgements pronounced at the end of the novel might at first appear to be the richest source of knowledge about Adolphe's character, since their goal is manifestly that of overall understanding. Yet they raise problems which may prove to be almost insurmountable: first, we are aware that the two characters who pronounce their judgements hardly knew Adolphe (the editor himself met him only once, and the correspondent can claim only to have known some of the participants in the story without having influenced its course); second, their judgements of Adolphe refer in the main to information we already have, and they do not provide any new psychological insights; third, the fact that they lead in opposite directions anyway implies that there can be no stable view of Adolphe on the evidence available. It is as though character-analysis in conventional terms can do no more than utter high-sounding abstractions or fall into empty moralizing. It does not impinge on the underlying motives.

Views of Adolphe within the narrative itself may, on the other hand, help us to pin down some of his characteristics more clearly. Even if these are often geared towards moral interpretation, they occasionally provide insights which bear on the unfolding of the drama itself. Such is the case with Ellénore's comments to Adolphe in the posthumous letter, where we are given a genuine revelation about his behaviour:

> Ce que j'obtiens de mieux, c'est votre silence. Tant de dureté ne convient pas à votre caractère. Vous êtes bon; vos actions sont nobles et dévouées: mais quelles actions effaceraient vos paroles? (pp. 117-18)

This may at first reading puzzle us, for it is a facet of Adolphe's behaviour which his own analysis had not made as clear: on the contrary, he had looked upon his own taciturnity as sullen withdrawal rather than kindness, and he might have preferred to see his *actions* as cruel (such as the increased visits to the baron de T***) and his *words* as noble (the stirring 'Mes bras ne sont-ils pas ton unique asile?', p. 77). Yet further reflection confirms that Ellénore's judgement is probably about correct: there is noble action in Adolphe's accompanying her to Poland or in his solicitude as she approaches death; and there are cruel words when he tells her he no longer loves her, or (in a quite different context unknown to Ellénore herself) when he jokes about women with the baron de T***. In the event, this insight is borne out by some other reactions towards Adolphe in the story. One corroboration of it comes from his father who emphasizes the rift between words or thoughts on the one hand, and deeds on the other hand, when he writes of his son's behaviour: 'Je ne puis que vous plaindre de ce qu'avec votre esprit d'indépendance, vous faites toujours ce que vous ne voulez pas' (p. 86). It is further corroborated by a tactic which the baron de T*** employs: he puts into words what he knows lies beneath the surface of Adolphe's actions, and describes his own arguments as 'des raisonnements que vous répétez sans cesse à vous-même' (p. 87). Once again, we are told that Adolphe is 'saying' one thing and doing another, and that his actions are invariably more compliant than his words. From three separate sources we now have a similar assessment of Adolphe, and we are probably entitled to believe that something is established beyond doubt.

The symbiosis of conflicting tendencies is so central to the philosophical vision of the novel that it comes almost as a relief to see it clearly and unambiguously pinpointed as being one of the hero's own characteristics. Yet this reflection of the epistemology of the text at the level of character presentation also raises problems. Whilst the overall view seems to be that the conflicting aspects of every issue make categorical judgement unviable, the hero's own hesitation between different possibilities is, as far as other characters are concerned, a weakness and a moral failing, not a philosophical strength. How, then, must we judge Adolphe? Do we align our view with that of the characters within the text and condemn him, or do we adopt the more open-ended system implicit in the novel as a whole and see his indecision as a mark of true awareness? In fact, as soon as we find ourselves putting such questions there is no further option: for we have been 'caught out' trying to decide between equal possibilities, and to exclude either one from our reasoning would be a falsification; thus we find ourselves infected too by the ambivalence of the text, and if we wish to have a means of judging the character of Adolphe we will have to seek it elsewhere.

In a sense, it is when Adolphe takes a detached look at his earlier self at the beginning of the story that we learn most about him. Here we learn of several qualities of the hero's character; but we also learn of a specific pattern of behaviour, which is his contradictory reaction to society. On the one hand, he exacts vengeance on its harsh but superficial judgements, but on the other hand he respects his father's wishes as far as his own education is concerned and looks to follow a conventionally respectable path in the world. Now this insight into his social attitudes is of great importance, for it is an aspect of the hero which is clearly visible throughout the novel and which increases the knowledge we have of him from other sources.

The contradiction inherent in Adolphe's perception of society is apparent even at the outset of his seduction campaign, when he remembers his father's 'système assez immoral' (p. 42) in relation to the female sex. Adolphe is prepared to share the hypocrisy of society (which solicits the favours of women, then condems their follies) even if his own moral sense tells him it is wrong. More even than his moral sense, his very sensitivity to Ellénore's charms is itself enough to destroy his illusion of being a cold seducer ('chaque mot qu'elle disait me semblait revêtu d'une grâce inexplicable', p. 46). Yet this initial conflict between social callousness on the one hand, and moral sense or human sensitivity on the other hand, will remain throughout Adolphe's relationship with Ellénore. Never does he have the courage to make of his liaison a social showpiece, thus classifying Ellénore publicly as his mistress, as did the comte de P***; but nor does he have the courage to conduct his relationship outside society's jurisdiction, and he finds (quite against his wishes) something of the libertine's secretiveness in his own behaviour. The result is that he feels excluded from society and yearns for reintegration into it. If he does rebel against society, then that rebellion remains superficial. Adolphe is basically conventional, a respecter of society's rules despite criticism of its over-simplified judgements. This is the opposite mixture from the one we find in Ellénore: she is unconventional, yet chooses to judge her conduct by the prevailing social standards none the less.

In Adolphe's attitude towards society we can, then, focus clearly on what is individual to him, the more so since we have the contrast of other characters' attitudes. We thus find confirmation of what is diagnosed at a different level by his father, the baron de T*** and Ellénore, namely that there is persistent and debilitating conflict within him. But this may lead us to ask further questions, which as yet remain unanswered. Where does the conflict stem from? Is it possible to find its causes and to see its inner workings? Is there a means of seeing beneath the surface? It would be asking a great deal of the narrating Adolphe to expect clear answers to such questions, especially since plausibility requires that he retain in some measure his earlier characteristics. At this point, an entirely different method of analysis is called for.

ii. The psychocritical approach. Recent studies of the character of Adolphe from a psychocritical perspective *(12, 33)* have revealed important insights. Although the methodological framework of such studies lies quite outside the terms of reference of Constant's novel, its application reveals an accurate intuition on his part of what was later to be systematically demonstrated by Freud and others.

The first and most striking claim of the psychocritical approach is that, far from being the victim of an incapacity to have feelings, Adolphe is on the contrary ravaged by an excess of feelings (see especially *33,* pp. 35-40). This is a direct contradiction of what Adolphe himself explicitly states ('Je n'étais soutenu par aucune impulsion qui partît du cœur', p. 69) and from it are derived all the other claims of the psychocritical reading. The discrepancy of interpretation between the critics and Adolphe himself is, of course, easily explained: as Han Verhoeff suggests, it is a matter of principle not to accept the narrator's account of his liaison at its face value, and the tone of guilt and self-reproach which characterizes it must be seen, like the confession of a subject of psychoanalysis, as a cover-up to prevent admission of the real issues (*33,* pp. 23-25). By blaming himself for not having strong enough feelings, Adolphe is avoiding confrontation with feelings of overwhelming power, and he has apparently found the perfect alibi. The task of the psychocritical approach will, therefore, be to look at what is left out of his account, and to ask why.

The most glaringly obvious, yet never-mentioned fact in the narrator's account of his childhood is the absence of the mother. Did she perhaps die in childbirth, or at some later stage? Did she live separately from Adolphe's father? Did Adolphe know her? Could he have been an 'enfant naturel' raised by the father alone? We will search the text in vain for answers to such questions: they simply are not there, and we are thus faced with a complete blank in a matter which

is surely of crucial importance (bearing as it does on both
the father's and Adolphe's attitude towards women). Compare this, for example, with the situation in *Manon Lescaut*
where, although the mother is absent, reference is at least
made to her and we are not left so completely in the dark
about the parental couple.

The psychocritical approach thus speculates that there is
unconscious censorship on the part of the narrating
Adolphe, and points out that there are clues in his attitude
towards Ellénore that he is in some way looking to replace
the mother-figure and to resolve his early complexes. The
age difference between the lovers is discreetly suggested at
the outset to the novel ('...quoiqu'elle ne fût plus de la
première jeunesse', says Adolphe in his very first reference
to her, p. 43), together with the element of maternal condescension on Ellénore's part which comes of her seniority.
The narrator tells us that, after his first declaration of love,
'Ellénore vit dans ma lettre ce qu'il était naturel d'y voir, le
transport passager d'un homme qui avait dix ans de moins
qu'elle, dont le cœur s'ouvrait à des sentiments qui lui
étaient encore inconnus' (p. 48). Beyond the difference in
age, one might wish to see in Adolphe's overall attitude to
Ellénore further signs of a surrogate son-to-mother relationship: inconsistent in his behaviour towards her, he will
alternate between willing submission to her tenderness and
fitful attempts at independent self-affirmation. The oscilla-
tion is a typically immature pattern of behaviour which
'sounds out' different attitudes before reaching a stable
definition of self.

As for Adolphe's relationship with his father, it is clear
from his account that the establishment of normal, healthy
one-to-one contact is severely hampered by the father's
inability to construct open channels of communication. Far
from learning how to interact with others, Adolphe learns
only to repress his feelings and to see the presence of others
as an obstacle: 'Je m'accoutumai à renfermer en moi-même
tout ce que j'éprouvais, à ne former que des plans solitaires'
(p. 36). The father's failure becomes Adolphe's own failure;
the lid is kept tightly closed on the tumult of inner sensa-

tion, and a cold exterior is cultivated. The result is a split personality, incapable of expressing its own uniqueness in daily communication.

Adolphe is, then, doubly hampered in the early forma-tion of his character: first by the absence of a mother, second by the disastrous nature of his relationship with his father (prejudicial as this is to what psychologists call 'the definition of ego'). The relationship with Ellénore is built on these shaky foundations, and its undoing appears thus to be almost inevitable. What is surprising perhaps is that Adolphe does go some of the way in it towards a solution of his problems, for he learns to sense the reality of another human presence, and when Ellénore dies he does not wish to re-enter the solitary world of the imagination which, as a youth, he had craved for. Yet, for all the progress he makes, the original trauma of the loss of the mother is never confronted. Initially beheld as the 'mother recovered' – perhaps against the false principles of a paternal society – Ellénore is gradually abandoned and finally 'killed' at the end of the story. Now the death of Ellénore gives extra weight to the psychocritical theory of Adolphe's behaviour (see especially *12, passim,* and *13,* pp. 100-12 on this). If she is perceived as the mother-figure, then her 'killing' is the climax of the repressed inner drama. Is the re-enactment of the original trauma a form of displaced revenge (and a sign that Adolphe's behaviour has been governed by aggression throughout), or is it some kind of self-imposed therapy, a coming-to-terms with the unmentionable by repetition of it? Is it even, as two critics have at least suggested (*24,* pp. 257-64; *33,* pp. 117-20), a pre-emptive therapy on the part of the author himself, who is coming to terms via his literary creations with his own private traumas and the fear of causing irreparable damage in human relationships? Once again we are liable to find ourselves in the realm of speculation; but if the psychocritical approach does not provide the final answer, it does undoubtedly reveal a new and important dimension of the text.

iii. Hero and narrator. We have, in one sense, reached
the limits of our possibilities as far as the analysis of the
character of Adolphe is concerned. Having started in the
knowledge that the hero of a first-person novel is inevitably
elusive as a character, yet having discovered that certain
traits and manners can none the less be isolated, we have
been able to go beyond this and glimpse the secret inner
motivations unmentioned at the surface of the text. But this
in turn leads us full circle, for we find ourselves once again
without any clear indication as to how finally to judge
Adolphe. The psychocritical approach seems, in the last
analysis, to suggest that the author himself is too close to his
hero to be able to provide us with an appropriate framework
by which to assess him.

Is the hero's world then a totally enclosed one, which the
reader is obliged either to enter at the cost of moral detachment or to judge entirely on the basis of her or his own
values and assumptions? Between these two alternatives
there is, I think, another possibility which, if more elusive,
is the more acceptable since it is built into the narrative.
That possibility is offered by the narrating Adolphe who
reflects upon and re-enacts the events of his story, standing
(for a while at least) some way distant from his earlier,
participating self.

While some critics of *Adolphe* suggest that the identifica-
tion between hero and narrator is so close that any attempt
to separate the two is doomed to failure, others prefer to see
the narrating Adolphe as a detached observer of the past
who views events from a static vantage-point.[16] Surely the
truth is somewhere between these positions. On the one
hand, we are aware of an outside voice superimposing its
reflections on past events, sometimes even designating itself
by specific linguistic signs ('...une certaine absence d'abandon qu'aujourd'hui encore mes amis me reprochent', p. 37;

---

[16] For an example of the first argument, see William Holdheim, *Benjamin Constant,* London, Bowes and Bowes, 1961, p. 48; for an example of
the second, see Marian Hobson, 'Theme and structure in *Adolphe'*, *Modern
Language Review,* 66 (1971), 306.

'La pauvre Ellénore, je l'écris dans ce moment...', p. 103).
On the other hand, we know that the tendency towards
abstraction and generalization, which seems to be the chief
characteristic of the narrating voice, was already present in
the earlier Adolphe; and we will see too that the narrating
voice loses that faculty as the story progresses (for the maxims
become less frequent and the tone more emotional). This is
not a static, outside narrator; it is one who is disturbed by
the shock of contact with his former self and who, on
recounting his story, discovers that there are elements in it
which may not have been appreciated at the time. The
progress of the hero Adolphe towards increased weariness
with his mistress is countered by the progress of the narrating Adolphe towards increased awareness of what was of
real value in his relationship. We will need, then, to look at
the way in which the narrator's attitude changes in the
course of his story, for this is bound to affect the way we are
encouraged to judge his former conduct.

In the opening chapter, the narrator is at his most
detached. The measured analysis of his childhood, of his
relationship with his father, of his conversations with the
elderly woman and his first contacts with society, implies
very strongly that the events he is about to recount have no
further bearing on his present personality. We are inclined,
in these opening pages, to believe that there is such a
distance between the participating and the narrating
Adolphe as to make of them almost two separate characters.

From this perspective of extreme detachment, it becomes clear also what the narrating Adolphe's aim is: it is
one of complete explanation and assessment, with the implication that, if his past conduct is looked at in a sufficiently general manner, its ultimate moral consequences will be
understood. Certainly there is no question at this stage of
any sympathetic re-enactment of past events. The rift between past and present is made abundantly clear in the
central remark: 'Je ne veux point ici me justifier: j'ai
renoncé depuis longtemps à cet usage frivole et facile d'un
esprit sans expérience' (p. 40).

The highly detached tone of chapter one already begins to be modified by the narrating Adolphe at the beginning of chapter two. Paradoxically, this modification comes about through the use of what would seem to be the most detached of all forms of comment: the maxim. The nature of the maxims which now begin to infiltrate the narrative is such that, rather than assign blame or responsibility, they emphasize the complexity of human motivation and the need to understand it from within. The first is perhaps the most significant: 'Les sentiments de l'homme sont confus et mélangés...' (p. 42). Though Adolphe's goal of explaining his past and achieving a moral clarification of his errors has not changed, the emphasis from this point onwards begins subtly to shift. No longer will it be possible for him to stand outside that past, for if he is to understand it fully he must submit to its tensions and conflicts, reliving its contradictions from within without simplifying the issues. The almost cynical detachment of the earlier narrating Adolphe will henceforth gradually be discarded. But the dangers of the new enterprise, however honest it may be, are immediately apparent. To enter into the confusion of the past is to risk losing one's sense of direction, for it is to abandon the advantage of distance. The narrator's approach to his past will now mirror the whole view of language which is suggested in the novel: language cannot be a static representation of a stable reality; the interplay between word and deed is never-ending, and just as language undergoes perpetual modifications in its attempts to describe reality, so reality is transformed for its being enshrined in language. If the narrator is henceforth denied the ability to judge his past conduct, he is none the less making a step towards seeing the complexity of the truth. Let us now take some examples of the way this progression continues, first from the middle, and then from the later stages of the novel.

In chapter five, Adolphe describes his feelings of irresolution and horror at the thought of leaving Ellénore and returning to his father. The tone becomes increasingly emotional as he relives his promise to her to reunite two months later: 'Quel engagement n'aurais-je pas pris dans un moment où je la voyais lutter contre elle-même et contenir sa douleur!' (p. 72). The exclamatory style betrays his present uncertainty about how to judge his past conduct. But uncertainty will be shown in another way later in the same chapter, when Adolphe hesitates in his very analysis of events. Reflecting on his failure to find a means of rejoining Ellénore after the separation, he says: 'Peut-être, car il faut être sincère, peut-être je ne la désirais pas' (p. 37). He has progressed from knowing what his motives were and regretting them, to no longer even knowing what were his motives. He is discovering to his cost the truth of his own maxim about the complexity of human motives, and if he is learning something, it is that his past conduct *cannot* be judged.

The final chapters of the novel show the lapse of the narrator's original intentions into confusion and even despair. He tries unsuccessfully, for example, to explain to himself the change of attitude which he undergoes on leaving the baron de T***'s house: 'Je sortis en achevant ces paroles, mais qui m'expliquera par quelle mobilité le sentiment qui les dictait s'éteignit avant même que j'eusse fini de les prononcer?' (p. 89). Alongside the implicit appeal to an outsider to continue the analysis in his place, we find a tone of emotional exclamation and pained surprise. This rises to a climax in the closing lines of the eighth chapter, where the narrator refers to Ellénore's prediction that she will soon be in the grave. He proclaims: 'Malheureux! lorsqu'elle parlait ainsi, que ne m'y suis-je jeté moi-même avant elle!' (p. 102). His horror at what took place is surpassed only by his incomprehension at its occurring at all, and he finds himself having to admit that he simply cannot understand his own behaviour. Describing his reaction to suspicions voiced by Ellénore he will say: 'Accusé par elle, le croira-t-on? je ne m'occupai qu'à tout éluder. Je niai même, oui, je niai ce jour-là ce que j'étais déterminé à lui déclarer le lendemain' (p. 106).

What is striking in the development of Constant's narrator is that the transition should be so complete, with self-assurance giving way to bafflement. The narrator's silence at the end of the story, as the task of judgement is posthumously handed to Ellénore, is the inevitable result of this change. The contradictions of his enterprise are such that they become insoluble. The initial goal of moral clarification is totally undermined by the necessity to explain all, and in the absence of that goal there can be no further reason to speak. What is particularly striking, if the chronology of events is reconstructed, is that Adolphe does not break free of his taciturnity: when the editor meets him in the Italian inn (the meeting takes place, of course, *after* the writing of Adolphe's story), it is the quality which is most immediately apparent. Perhaps, then, it is the very telling of his story which destroys Adolphe. There is nothing in the course of his narration which changes except his own attitude, for the events in it were of the past even at the beginning of his account.

Looked at in this way, the evolution of Constant's narrator provides us with a perspective which, if it does not fully satisfy our desire to assess the character of Adolphe, does at least enable us to see why straight moral judgements cannot be made. For as the narrator tries to analyse his past action, he discovers that the very instrument of analysis is subject to distortion. As he himself says: 'La parole [est] toujours trop grossière et trop générale' (p. 42). This explains in part why the character of Adolphe remains so elusive, and in addition gives us an insight into Constant's vision of the world: absolute truth cannot be seen to exist, and moral analysis cannot wrest itself clear of the imperfections of language.

iv.   The positive lesson. There is a further dimension added to the character of Adolphe by the presence of the narrator, to which I wish now to return. This is the discovery, which emerges during the recounting of the story, of the positive and valuable side of the relationship despite its failure. It is because the narrator's account takes him in an unexpected direction that he ceases to look upon his past with the eye of a cynic and reveals in it an overall pattern which had quite escaped him.

The first moment of retrospective awareness about love comes as Adolphe is recounting the completion of his seduction of Ellénore. At the end of chapter three we read the exclamation: 'Malheur à l'homme qui, dans les premiers moments d'une liaison d'amour, ne croit pas que cette liaison doit être éternelle!' (p. 59). Now this may be read in a variety of ways. Is the narrator suggesting that there was already, at the very inception of his relationship with Ellénore, a hint of doubt in his own mind about its prospects? Is he suggesting that there is misfortune on anybody *else* who may harbour such doubts, but that he himself was free of them? Or could his attitude be a blend of these two possibilities, meaning that although he *now* sees that there could have been doubt in his mind, *at the time* he was not aware of it? Whichever of these readings one chooses – and perhaps we are not in the end meant to opt – the effect of Adolphe's remark is to provide for the first time in the work the reflection that, even if love failed, it may not have been potentially less genuine for that failure. The reflection is reinforced by what follows it almost immediately at the beginning of chapter four, with the lyrical yet detailed evocation of those magical qualities of love in its first instants.

So far, the narrator's comments have been confined to the intensity of new love. Yet one of Adolphe's main problems is his inability to prolong that intensity. As critics have pointed out (*9*, p. 26; *25*, p. 260) he is, at the outset of his adventure, a creature who has no real sense of duration. Attracted by the magical instant, he cannot imagine the gradual development and growth of mutual feelings through time. This sense of duration is, however, painfully acquired as the relationship with Ellénore pursues its course, and it is the narrator, emotional and confused though he may be in the revival of his past, who is able to pinpoint it.

As he recalls his first departure from Ellénore, the narrator is already aware of how time had ensnared him in his relationship: 'Il y a dans les liaisons qui se prolongent quelque chose de si profond! Elles deviennent une partie si intime de notre existence!' (pp. 72-73). If his remark here is to some extent a rationalization of his own weakness in the circumstances, it nevertheless contains a thought which will not be lost. During the journey to Poland, Adolphe again reflects on the density with which the passing of time endows even the unsteadiest of relationships, with shared memories increasing the sense of intimacy (p. 85). And again at the conclusion, the novel returns to the theme of time shared with another, and through the anguish and bitterness of failure we see the narrator's awareness (a little distorted perhaps) of worth:

> Ce fut alors que j'éprouvai la douleur déchirante et toute l'horreur de l'adieu sans retour. [...] Combien elle me pesait, cette liberté que j'avais tant regrettée! Combien elle manquait à mon cœur, cette dépendance qui m'avait révolté souvent! Naguère toutes mes actions avaient un but; j'étais sûr, par chacune d'elles, d'épargner une peine ou de causer un plaisir. [...] J'étais libre, en effet, je n'étais plus aimé: j'étais étranger pour tout le monde. (pp. 116-17)

Although Adolphe's attention is focused on the pain of his present situation without Ellénore, the implied value which makes the reflection possible is that of the sense of real contact achieved by living through time with another human being. It is because he has come to an awareness of such contact that Adolphe now feels its absence.

There has thus been a major change in Adolphe's attitude. Initially accepting contact with others in sporadic bursts only, he comes to recognize through his enforced intimacy with Ellénore the value of regular, continuous communication. As Georges Poulet puts it, the story is about the awakening of a true sense of morality in Adolphe, as he discovers that sincerity with another must be placed on a firmer basis than that of joyful spontaneity: 'En découvrant Ellénore en tant que personne par la souffrance qu'il lui cause, Adolphe découvre la valeur de la personne, et se hausse ainsi jusqu'à la moralité' (*26*, p. 87).

If it is true that the telling of the story is what brings to the surface and reinforces Adolphe's awareness of the worth of human contact, then we begin to understand why its implications remain so elusive. Not only does this positive message conflict with the intentions of the narrator at the outset, it conflicts also in a large degree with the events themselves. Some might wish to conclude that the retrospective discovery of value is, in fact, no more than a self-exonerating tactic by the narrator. Such a view seems to me less than sympathetic, for it rests on the assumption that Adolphe is deliberately falsifying his case; if we accepted it, we should soon be arguing that he is a liar, and that would lead nowhere. Adolphe does acknowledge at an early stage that his love for Ellénore is wanting ('Je suis convaincu que, si j'avais eu de l'amour pour Ellénore...', p. 69); but the overall failure of love does not of its own accord preclude the ideal of a genuinely mutual relationship, and there are, as the beginning of chapter four shows, moments of true delight shared by the couple. For the narrator to have ignored this positive strand would have been to betray the truth. In Constant's view of things, opposites may exist alongside each other without necessarily being irreconcilable.

Conclusion

To look at the manner in which the hero of *Adolphe* is presented is to discover, at yet another level, the ambivalence of Constant's response to the moral issues he evokes. As the narrator learns, a categorical and detached approach to his past experience, though desirable, is unmanageable. Sincerity requires that he should recreate the subjective ideals implicit in his actions and give them due weight in his analysis. But whilst he is in the end foiled in his attempts to grapple with such conflicting demands, a positive message remains which is surely the author's own: human experience must be accepted as unfathomably complex before even a semblance of honesty can be achieved in the assessment of it.

Here we find ourselves at the very heart of Constant's subject, for the question which is being asked throughout his novel is whether there is an essential truth to be revealed through the act of confession. Underlying this general question are two more specific ones. First, are the demands of society such that authentic expression of feeling is rendered impossible? And second, does language itself create insurmountable barriers to the true perception of the inner self?

Before Constant, Jean-Jacques Rousseau had addressed himself to similar problems; but whereas for Rousseau self-awareness is the door to true self-discovery, Constant's world is marked by the absence of such certainties. There are no emotions powerful or instinctive enough to be considered 'natural'. Even pity, the most spontaneous feeling experienced by Adolphe, is produced partly by his own sense of guilt: it is far from being that 'pur mouvement de la nature, antérieur à toute reflexion' which Rousseau sees it

as in his *Discours sur l'origine de l'inégalité.*[17] And yet, if
the presence of a reflective mind corrupts even this the most
powerful of emotions for Constant, he does not conclude
that civilized man is thereby condemned to falsehood and
sham. Rather, he suggests that human behaviour, as well as
the analysis of it, contains a mixture of motives, and that
beyond the posturing and self-interest which society inevitably encourages there may also be fragments of integrity
and purity. In his prefaces to *Adolphe,* he draws attention to
the existence of genuine emotions even in men who pride
themselves on callous feats of seduction; and Adolphe
himself discovers, when pursuing such a goal, that the
presence of Ellénore produces in him powerful feelings
which threaten the whole edifice of his cynical convictions.

Constant's answer to the central questions of his novel is,
then, a qualified one. No simple truths can be expressed
about our actions, since these are a mosaic of conflicting
impulses in which society and language are themselves
constituent elements. This being the case, the novelist's task
must be to expose the complex workings of human behaviour within its social and linguistic context. Thus society is
represented in *Adolphe* as part of the very fabric of man's
existence, without which he would have no substance at all.
Language too, which is after all a social instrument, becomes an inextricable element in the development of emotions, and the speaking of words itself produces some of the
climaxes in the novel (most notably Ellénore's 'Vous n'avez
que de la pitié'). As Todorov has said in his study of
language in *Adolphe,* words often exist in a 'synecdochal'
relationship to the thing they designate (*31,* p. 102): that is
to say, they are a part of the whole, not an outside and
independent entity or an objective tool of analysis.[18] Indeed,
Constant seems to be saying that any attempt to view man

---

[17] Jean-Jacques Rousseau, *Discours sur les sciences et les arts, Discours
sur l'origine et les fondements de l'inégalité parmi les hommes,* Paris,
Garnier-Flammarion, 1971, p. 197.

[18] Todorov has recently extended his theories to cover other aspects of
Constant's world-view in an article entitled 'Benjamin Constant, politique
et amour', *Poétique,* 56 (1983), pp. 485-510.

outside the context of his society and its language is a
falsification, for he exists by and through them. Where
many Romantics look for the essence of human nature at a
purely spiritual or metaphysical level, Constant strikes a
somewhat different note by locating it resolutely at the level
of social interaction.

And yet, for all its concentration on the concrete problems of a human relationship, *Adolphe* also leaves us with a
powerful impression of man's frailty in the face of the
absolute. As he describes the death of Ellénore, Adolphe
reflects: 'Ma surprise n'est pas que l'homme ait besoin
d'une religion; ce qui m'étonne, c'est qu'il se croie jamais
assez fort, assez à l'abri du malheur pour oser en rejeter une'
(p. 115). Does this mean that religion offers a positive
consolation in Constant's world, or is it merely a straw to be
clutched at in desperation? Is death a release, the awareness
of which helps us to transcend the concerns of the ego, or is
it a finality in the face of which religion is no more than a
perfunctory attempt to claw back some hope? Constant
answers in a characteristic manner: it can be either of these
things, since the problem alters according to the way in
which it is subjectively perceived by the individual. His
attention in *Adolphe* focuses less on the general philosophical problem of death than on the manner in which the
awareness of it is altered by, and alters, the consciousness of
his characters. There are two points where this becomes
especially clear.

The first is the passage describing Adolphe's night of
wandering at the end of chapter seven. Having achieved a
momentary peace as he beholds the countryside around
him, the hero falls, in the latter stages of his meditation, into
a negative and sombre fatalism; the consoling idea of death
becomes, in the end, a simple wish to escape the suffering of
life (pp. 93-94). Adolphe's own inner agitation colours and
distorts his thoughts about death, and his thoughts about
death fuel that agitation in turn. (See *27* for an extended
analysis of this passage.) But precisely the opposite process
occurs in the other passage where death, and the religious
response to it, is evoked: this is the final scene which

describes Ellénore's fatal sickness. Although there are signs
of continued agitation in Ellénore as she hovers fitfully on
the edge of life (such as that desperate moment when she
fails to find Adolphe's letter among her papers), the overall
mood is one of firm acceptance of what she knows to be
inevitable. Given this state of mind, she finds strength, not
anxiety, in her religion: she is able to reject any possibility
of a continuation of her relationship with Adolphe, and
makes absolution her final concern. Thus her attitude
towards death is altogether more positive than was Adolphe's; and this is both because her new mood makes her
more receptive to religion, and because religion itself in-
duces in her a state of serenity. To the last, Constant points
out the dynamic interplay between external forces and the
inner life of the individual.

If we are looking to *Adolphe* for a stable set of precepts
on love, society, language, religion or death, then we are in
the end liable to be disappointed, despite the author's
promisingly philosophical turn of phrase. The work touches
on many themes, but it is in the nature of Constant's
approach to show that their significance is relative to an
ever-changing context, and he prefers to expose the enigmas
of human motives rather than to pronounce moral judgement. Whereas eighteenth-century novelists had often
sought to justify their works by pointing out in prefaces
their instructive value, Constant can do no more than pay
lip-service to such a tradition: for his world is one in which
moral and philosophical dilemmas are ultimately seen as
insoluble, and where the anguish and self-doubt of modern
man are expressed to perfection. But his novel is far from
offering the depressing and negative message that some see
in it. Rather, it asserts that the very recognition of human
frailty provides the way forward, and that man at least has
the will to seek for truth, if not always the means to find it.

Select Bibliography

I. EDITIONS

1. Constant, Benjamin, *Œuvres,* texte présenté et annoté par Alfred Roulin, Paris, Gallimard, Bibliothèque de la Pléiade, 1957.
2. ———, *Adolphe,* édition historique et critique par Gustave Rudler, Manchester University Press, 1919.
3. ———, *Adolphe,* chronologie et introduction par Antoine Adam, Paris, Garnier-Flammarion, 1965.
4. ———, *Adolphe,* ed. Jacques-Henry Bornecque, Paris, Garnier, 1968.
5. ———, *Adolphe, anecdote trouvée dans les papiers d'un inconnu,* ed. W. Andrew Oliver, London, Macmillan, 1968.
6. ———, *Adolphe, suivi du Cahier rouge et de Poèmes inédits,* ed. Jean Mistler, Paris, Livre de Poche, 1972.
7. ———, *Adolphe, Le Cahier rouge, Cécile,* ed. Alfred Roulin, Paris, Folio (Gallimard, 1957).
8. ———, *Adolphe, anecdote trouvée dans les papiers d'un inconnu,* ed. Paul Delbouille, Paris, Les Belles Lettres, 1977.

II. CRITICAL WORKS

9. Alexander, Ian W., *Benjamin Constant: 'Adolphe',* London, Edward Arnold, 1973.
10. Baguley, David, 'The role of letters in Constant's *Adolphe', Forum for Modern Language Studies,* 11 (1975), 29-35.
11. Bowman, Frank Paul, 'Nouvelles lectures d'*Adolphe',* in *Annales Benjamin Constant,* 1, Geneva, Droz, 1980, 27-42.
12. Brady-Papadopoulou, Valentini, 'The killing of the "mother" in Constant's *Adolphe', Neophilologus,* 65 (1981), 6-14.
13. Charles, Michel, 'Adolphe ou l'inconstance', in *Rhétorique de la lecture,* Paris, Seuil, 1977, pp. 215-47.
14. Delbouille, Paul, *Genèse, structure et destin d"Adolphe',* Paris, Les Belles Lettres, 1971.
15. Fairlie, Alison, 'The art of Constant's *Adolphe:* the stylization of experience', *Modern Language Review,* 62 (1967), 31-47.
16. ———, 'The art of Constant's *Adolphe:* creation of character', *Forum for Modern Language Studies,* 2 (1966), 253-63.

17. Fairlie, Alison, 'The art of Constant's *Adolphe:* structure and style', *French Studies,* 20 (1966), 226-42.

(The essays by Alison Fairlie, together with four further studies on *Adolphe,* may be found in the collective volume of her articles on nineteenth-century authors, *Imagination and Language,* Cambridge University Press, 1981).

18. Gonin, Eve, *Le Point de vue d'Ellénore: une réécriture d"Adolphe',* Paris, José Corti, 1981.

19. Jallat, Jeannine, 'Adolphe, la parole et l'autre', *Littérature,* 2 (1971), 71-88.

20. King, Norman, 'Structure et stratégies d'*Adolphe',* in *Benjamin Constant, Madame de Staël et le Groupe de Coppet, Actes du deuxième congrès de Lausanne, 1980,* Lausanne, Institut Benjamin Constant, Oxford, The Voltaire Foundation, 1982, pp. 267-85.

21. Le Hir, Yves, 'Lignes de force sur l'imagination de B. Constant dans *Adolphe', Convivium,* 26 (1958), 328-31.

22. Mercken-Spass, Godeliève, *Alienation in Constant's 'Adolphe': an exercise in structural thematics,* Bern, Peter Lang, 1977.

23. Morrison, Ian R., 'Emotional involvement and the failure of analysis in *Adolphe', Neophilologus,* 60 (1976), 334-41.

24. Oliver, Andrew, *Benjamin Constant: écriture et conquête du moi,* Paris, Minard, 1970.

25. Poulet, Georges, *Etudes sur le temps humain,* Edinburgh University Press, 1949.

26. ———, *Benjamin Constant par lui-même,* Paris, Seuil, 1968.

27. ———, 'Benjamin Constant et le thème de l'abnégation', in *Actes du Congrès Benjamin Constant, Lausanne, octobre 1967,* Geneva, Droz, 1968, pp. 153-59.

28. Schilling, Robert, 'Encadrement du récit et structure d'*Adolphe', Bulletin de la Faculté des Lettres de Mulhouse,* 4 (1971-72), 49-58.

29. Scott, M., 'The Romanticism of *Adolphe', Nottingham French Studies,* V, 2 (1967), 58-66.

30. Thomas, Ruth P., 'The ambiguous narrator of *Adolphe', Romance Notes,* 14 (1972-73), 486-95.

31. Todorov, Tzvetan, 'La Parole selon Constant', in *Poétique de la prose,* Paris, Seuil, 1971, pp. 100-17.

32. Turnell, Martin, *The Novel in France,* New York, Plainview, 1951 (repr. 1972).

33. Verhoeff, Han, *'Adolphe' et Constant: une étude psychocritique,* Paris, Klincksieck, 1976.

III.   BIBLIOGRAPHICAL

34.   Hofmann, Etienne et al., *Bibliographie analytique des écrits sur Benjamin Constant (1796-1980),* Lausanne, Institut Benjamin Constant, Oxford, The Voltaire Foundation, 1980.
35.   Lowe, David K., *Benjamin Constant: an annotated bibliography of critical editions and studies, 1946-1978,* London, Grant and Cutler, Research Bibliographies and Checklists, No. 26, 1979.

IV.   RECENT ITEMS

36.   Constant, Benjamin, *Adolphe, anecdote trouvée dans les papiers d'un inconnu,* ed. C.P. Courtney, Oxford, Blackwell, 1989.
37.   Spencer, Michael, ' "L'on se racontait mon histoire". Embedding, Narration and Judgement in *Adolphe', French Forum*, 12 (1987), 175-85.
38.   Unwin, Timothy, 'Maxims and Generalizations in the Novel: Constant and Flaubert', *Journal of European Studies*, 17 (1987), 167-77.
39.   Wood, Dennis, *Constant: 'Adolphe'*, Cambridge, CUP, 1987.

CRITICAL GUIDES TO FRENCH TEXTS

edited by
Roger Little, Wolfgang van Emden, David Williams